THE AZUSA STREET REVIVAL

THE HOLY SPIRIT IN AMERICA 100 YEARS

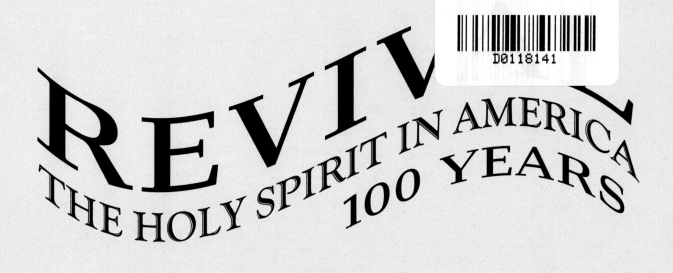

SPECIAL CENTENNIAL EDITION

Charisma HOUSE

A STRANG COMPANY

Most Strang Communications/Charisma House/Siloam/Realms/ FrontLine products are available at special quantity discounts for bulk purchase for sales promotions, premiums, fund-raising, and educational needs. For details, write Strang Communications/Charisma House/Siloam/Realms, 600 Rinehart Road, Lake Mary, Florida 32746, or telephone (407) 333-0600.

The Azusa Street Revival—Special Centennial Edition

TBN Special Edition

Eddie Hyatt, Author

Joel Kilpatrick, General Editor

Terry Clifton, Designer

Published by Charisma House

A Strang Company

600 Rinehart Road

Lake Mary, Florida 32746

www.charismahouse.com

Unless otherwise noted, all Scripture quotations are from the New King James Version of the Bible. Copyright © 1979, 1980, 1982 by Thomas Nelson, Inc., publishers. Used by permission.

BROADCASTING THE
GOOD NEWS
TRINITY BROADCASTING NETWORK

F ROM SMALL BEGINNINGS IN A RENTED STUDIO IN 1973, THE TRINITY BROADCASTING
NETWORK (TBN), UNDER THE LEADERSHIP OF PAUL AND JAN CROUCH, HAS BECOME
THE WORLD'S LARGEST RELIGIOUS NETWORK AND AMERICA'S MOST-WATCHED FAITH
CHANNEL. BY SOME ESTIMATES IT IS THE SEVENTH LARGEST TELEVISION NETWORK OF ANY KIND
IN THE WORLD. BILLIONS HAVE TUNED IN TO TBN, AND AT LEAST 25 MILLION PEOPLE HAVE COME
TO FAITH IN JESUS THROUGH TBN'S MINISTRY.

WHEN THEY BEGAN

TBN founder Paul Crouch was born in 1934 and raised in the home of missionary and pastor Andrew Crouch. Andrew had been a gambler and was playing poker one night in a smoke-filled poolroom in South Dakota when, according to his account, he looked up and saw the devil sitting across from him. Frightened, Andrew saddled his horse and rode back to Iowa, where he surrendered his life to Jesus and to the ministry. He eventually became one of the founders of the Assemblies of God fellowship.

At age twelve, son Paul began tinkering with a mass of radio wires and equipment in a friend's basement. He spent hundreds of hours on the transmitter and the "ham rig," and at age fifteen, Crouch passed the Federal Communications Commission (FCC) test and became a licensed ham radio operator.

In 1952, when Paul was eighteen, his grandmother told him, "God is calling you

into the ministry." Paul never doubted it. After finishing high school, he attended Central Bible Institute in Springfield, Missouri. There he formed an amateur radio club. After scrounging up tubes, condensers, resistors, and 50 watts of power, KCBI was born. On its official sign-on night, after the national anthem, the historic words that

would later become Paul's signature greeting crackled through the wires—"Hello, world!"

In summer 1956, at a church in Rapid City, South Dakota, Paul was smitten by the sight of a belle from Georgia—Jan Bethany, whose father Edgar Bethany had founded Southeastern Bible College of the Assemblies of God in Lakeland, Florida, and now pastored the leading Assemblies of God church in the Southeast in Columbus, Georgia. Paul began courting her, and eventually they were married on August 25, 1957. The young couple accepted the posts of assistant pastors at First Assembly of God in Rapid City, South Dakota. Since the church could not fully support them financially, Paul found work as a radio announcer at KRSD AM 1340, which eventually became KRSD-TV Channel 7. There Paul learned the

ON SET
Paul on the set of the Assemblies of God TV and Film Production studio in Burbank.

EARLY BROADCASTS
(left) Paul Crouch at KCBI, the on-campus radio station he helped build at Central Bible College in Springfield, Missouri.

READY TO LAUNCH
(right) Paul and Jan help ready the rented TBN studio for its first broadcast of the Praise the Lord program on May 28, 1973.

basics of television broadcasting in what he described later as his boot-camp experience.

The Crouches then moved to Muskegon, Michigan, where they served for two years as assistant pastors at Central Assembly of God. There the Crouches received a call that would change their lives. Paul was told about a new TV and film production center the Assemblies of God was building in Burbank, California. He was offered the position of manager, which he accepted, and on Thanksgiving Day 1961 he and Jan and their young two sons, Paul Jr. and Matthew, moved to California. Paul would manage the Assemblies of God TV and Film Production Center in Burbank for nearly five years.

The Assemblies of God moved the production center to Springfield, Missouri, and the Crouches stayed in California. Paul managed a radio station in Corona, where he received an in-the-trenches education in FCC law and business management. Then, in 1971, Ray Schoch, pastor of Faith Center church in Glendale, asked Paul to manage his radio and television stations. Schoch had a vision for a TV station that was solely devoted to Christian television. KHOF-TV Channel 30 was on the air, and Crouch helped manage the first television station that devoted 100 percent of its programming to Christian television.

HOST AND PIONEER
An early photo of Paul hosting the Behind the Scenes *program. The table on the right was part of Paul and Jan's home bedroom set.*

Times were exciting at KHOF-TV, but one night while driving out of the parking lot of Hollywood High School, Paul heard the voice of God say, "I release you from your ministry at KHOF-TV." After handing in his resignation, Paul contacted the owner of KBSA-TV to check on the status of a UHF station that was next to the main TV stations in Los Angeles. To Paul's surprise, Channel 46 had been off the air. He signed a series of contracts, and three months later, on May 28, the TBN era was born.

IT'S OFFICIAL
On August 2, 1974, Paul picked up the Western Union telegram from the FCC granting TBN's first television license for Channel 40 in Southern California.

SUCCESS AND TRIALS

TBN first aired from Santa Ana, California, with one borrowed camera, two folding chairs, and a Sears shower curtain for a backdrop. Paul, Jan, and a dedicated group of volunteers scrambled to overcome financial and technical obstacles to get on the air. It was the initial fulfillment of a calling the Crouches had received just three months earlier—a vision to build a Christian television network that would one day take the gospel to the world.

By November 1973, TBN had held its first telethon, and more than three thousand people claimed salvation through the station's ministry. Then, in late 1973, a pastor bought KBSA out from under Crouch. The fledging Trinity Broadcasting Network was about to come to an end, but after a time of agonizing prayer, Paul heard what he calls a "still, small voice" tell him to call a local Southern California broadcaster who owned the license for Channel 40. Unbeknownst to Paul, the owner had decided to sell the license for Channel 40 that very day. Crouch purchased the station, and TBN was back on the air with four times the power and double the population coverage as before.

In August 1974 the Federal Communications Commission approved TBN's license, and in 1978 the FCC granted a permit that allowed TBN to broadcast its signal by satellite. Licensing, though, would be a continual struggle for TBN. In the 1980s the network was plagued by competing applications for its licenses and a license challenge from the FCC. Several times the future of the network hung in the balance, but in each case TBN prevailed.

TBN grew during the 1980s, and by 1994 it had 450 stations and affiliates. The 1992 Cable Television Consumer Protection and Competition Act gave it the right to be carried on local cable systems, which meant access to millions more homes.

TBN was also quick to utilize new technologies. In 1995 TBN launched TBN .org, offering a constant presence on the World Wide Web. In 1996 the network began broadcasting on the Dish Network.

(top to bottom) In 1978, Paul, Jan, and hundreds of TBN partners prayed over and dedicated the new satellite station. TBN now reaches the world through its network of fifty-three international satellites. A photo from TBN's first family Christmas TV special in 1973. Paul and Jan are pictured with sons Matt (left) and Paul Jr. The set was decorated with Christmas cards sent by TBN's early partners. TBN soon outgrew its Santa Ana studio, and by 1975 had purchased property for its new home in Tustin, California.

The next year, DIRECTV added TBN to its service. Today, TBN is affiliated with all major cable and satellite companies.

In 2004 TBN announced its shift from analog to digital television, a transition overseen by Paul Crouch Jr. With digital television, TBN viewers will see TBN programs and channels with high-quality, crystal-clear pictures. Digital television also makes "multicasting" more than one channel possible, meaning that viewers will have access to all five of TBN's channels. TBN's shift to digital television is consistent with its vision of providing innovative programming around the world.

GLOBAL GROWTH

(counter-clockwise from top) Paul demonstrates TBN multicasting capabilities at a multicast distribution center in London. Paul in Bombay, India. TBN covers roughly half of India through cable and satellite. Rooftop satellite receiving dishes fill the skyline in Cairo, Egypt. TBN covers the entire Middle East via the Hotbird 6 satellite. Paul gives his signature "thumbs up" and "Hello, world" as he stands at the crossroads of the world sign in Reykjavik, Iceland.

TBN'S ORGANIZATION AND MISSION

TBN features more original and exclusive programs than any other faith channel. TBN also remains viewer supported, commercial free, and debt free. It operates a worldwide television network for a fraction of the cost of other U.S.-based networks and with fewer staff. It provides programming for the entire family, based in values of faith in God, love of family, and patriotic pride.

TBN has maintained a rare level of trust with its viewers. By proudly promoting traditional values and faith, and by remaining consistent since 1973, TBN has earned viewers' longtime loyalty. There have been no name or format changes, no advertisements, no paid infomercials, or no off-net reruns. When viewers tune in, whether they are longtime viewers or first-time viewers, they find positive Christian programming that offers hope and encouragement. Because TBN has held to the same goal for three decades, people have come to rely on the network, and many lives have been changed as a result.

TBN has experienced great continuity within its leadership structure. The network today is still under the direction of its founders, Paul and Jan Crouch. While they remain actively involved with the managing and strategic vision of TBN, Paul and Jan have increasingly relied on their sons, Paul Jr. and Matt, to share the responsibilities of operating the network.

INTERVIEWS
(right, top to bottom) Paul and Jan with the "voice of TBN," veteran Hollywood actor Efrem Zimbalist Jr. Efrem has announced the station breaks for the TBN network for more than thirty years.
Paul and Jan interview Billy Graham during his 2004 crusade at the Pasadena Rose Bowl.
Paul Sr. and Paul Jr. attended the Benny Hinn service in Bangalore, India, with three million other people.
Matt Crouch with Paul Sr. and Benny Hinn on the Praise the Lord set in Costa Mesa, California.

ALL THE WORLD
(top, l-r) Paul places the entire Bible—in microform—on board the Galaxy 5 satellite prior to its launch in 1991. Paul on TBN's TV tower in Bethlehem, Palestine. Some time after this photo was taken, the tower was destroyed by terrorists.

"We did not have a clue that TBN would expand to what it is today. We felt that one small station in Los Angeles was enough, but when we saw the enthusiastic response to the body of Christ, we began to seek out other stations....All those years we knew we were watching a miracle in progress, but that miracle just keeps moving forward."

—*Paul Crouch Sr.*

EUROPE
Paul on a rooftop in Lisbon, Portugal. TBN is on fifty-three satellite channels, reaching virtually the entire world with the gospel.

NEW PROGRAMMING DEVELOPMENTS

TBN programs appeal to a wide variety of viewers, and TBN continues to be the undisputed leader in producing original Christian programs, including gospel and contemporary Christian music concerts from the most popular artists, live coverage of major Christian events, and health and nutrition programs featuring the most up-to-date information and advice available from leading experts who take a faith-based approach to health and wellness.

Now, after decades of building studios and transmission towers around the world, TBN is upgrading its programming to include even better movies, documentaries, music shows, concerts, Bible study programs, reality shows, and more. TBN plans to eventually offer sitcoms and dramas that will reach a broader mainstream audience with the highest quality programming matched with contemporary content that nurtures family values and upholds spiritual beliefs.

In service of this goal, TBN recently launched four digital networks that are now available.

JCTV is a fully digital network geared toward teens and young adults. JCTV features round-the-clock, cutting-edge Christian music videos, reality and game shows, relevant talk programs, comedy programs, extreme sports, and much more.

The Church Channel is the only network featuring America's most popular church services from a wide variety of Protestant and Catholic congregations, broadcast twenty-four hours a day.

TBN Enlace USA, America's premier Spanish language faith network, offers

ACTION
Paul Crouch Jr. interviews Kirk Cameron on TBN's new Praise the Lord *set in Hollywood. (far right) In 1999, TBN's second full-length feature film,* The Omega Code, *was released. Paul is pictured with son Matt interviewing* Omega Code *star Michael York at the movie premiere in Hollywood.*

viewers the best inspirational programs from Latin America and the most popular programs from TBN all in Spanish, twenty-four hours a day.

The Smile of a Child network offers safe, entertaining programs for children ages two to twelve, all day long.

TBN is also a recognized leader in the production of major Christian movies, including the highly acclaimed *The Omega Code*, produced by Matt Crouch. *The Omega Code* was a top ten feature film on its opening weekend. TBN has since released other successful films like *Megiddo*, *The Revolutionary*, *The Emissary*, and *The Champion*. Current film projects include the End-Time thriller *Six: The Mark Unleashed*, starring Stephen Baldwin and David White, and one of Christian cinema's most ambitious projects yet, the epic *One Night With the King*, set for release in 2006 and featuring screen legends Peter O'Toole and Omar Sharif.

Photo by Ralph Bizik and Eric Alley

In addition to its own movies, TBN has partnered with Cloud Ten Pictures to bring its highly popular End-Time movie series Left Behind, starring Kirk Cameron, to television. The End-Time series continues with the third installment *Left Behind: World at War.*

TBN has also built several tourist attractions. Trinity Music City, USA in Nashville offers TBN-produced concerts, dramas, seminars, and special events. Thousands of visitors come every week to this former estate of country music legend Conway Twitty, now converted into a complex that includes the two-thousand-seat Trinity Music City Church Auditorium. Crowds pack the house to attend the TBN-produced events.

HEADQUARTERS
Trinity Christian City International—home of TBN headquarters in Costa Mesa, California.
Photo by Ralph Bizik and Eric Alley

CHRISTMASTIME
(left and above) TBN's headquarters, Trinity Christian City International in Costa Mesa, California, aglow with a million lights to celebrate the birth of Jesus—the Light of the world.

TBN is on the cutting edge of technology with state-of-the-art virtual reality theaters at Trinity Music City, the International Production Center in Dallas, TBN headquarters in Costa Mesa, and the newest virtual reality theater in Miami. These fifty-seat theaters combine high-definition digital video technology with an exclusive forty-eight-channel digital audio system to showcase four original productions from TBN Films: *The Revolutionary*, parts I and II, portraying the life and miracles of Jesus Christ; *The Emissary*, depicting miraculous events from the Book of Acts and the life of Paul; and *The Omega Code.*

TRINITY MUSIC CITY
In 1997, Trinity Music City in Hendersonville, Tennessee, opened its doors. Formerly "Twitty City," home to country music star Conway Twitty, it is now a Christian tourist attraction featuring TBN-produced dramas, concerts, and special events, as well as the Praise the Lord *program and virtual reality theater.*

CONTINUING INFLUENCE

Recently, the *Church Report* named Paul Crouch the sixth most influential Christian in America, the second year Crouch has been recognized. *Church Report* called him an "internationally recognized visionary in the field of Christian television." Bishop T. D. Jakes, pastor of The Potter's House in Dallas, was selected as the nation's most influential Christian this year. Jakes' program, *The Potter's Touch*, is broadcast daily on TBN, and the popular pastor and speaker has guest-hosted TBN's *Praise the Lord* program.

PREACHING THE WORD
For more than thirty years, TBN's flagship program, Praise the Lord, *has featured some of the most dynamic ministers of our time, such as Bishop T. D. Jakes of The Potter's House in Dallas, Texas.*

Paul Crouch Jr. also made the *Church Report's* listing for the first time, coming in at number twenty-nine. He serves as vice president of administration for TBN and works closely with his father in the network's rapidly expanding reach into new family-friendly broadcasting formats.

TBN's *Praise the Lord* program remains the heart and soul of the TBN program lineup, offering a steady variety of guests, including Christian pastors, political leaders, top athletes, war heroes, movie stars, and other entertainers. As it always has been, *Praise the Lord* is broadcast "live" from TBN production facilities throughout the United States, including its newest Hollywood facility on the grounds of the legendary Hanna-Barbera Studios. Crouch calls the program "a little slice of small-town America every day—a friendly visit with neighbors on the front porch, and we're always talking about the most important thing in life—faith in God."

PRAISE THE LORD
(left, top to bottom) Tammy Faye Messner shares her powerful testimony with Paul Crouch Jr. on Praise the Lord. *Evangelist Jesse Duplantis preaches a soul-stirring message during a TBN Praise-a-Thon. Two pioneers of Christian television, Oral Roberts and Rex Humbard, join Benny Hinn on* Praise the Lord. *Christmas with the Crouches on* Praise the Lord.
(below) Paul is joined by Benny Hinn and a group of Egyptian pastors as they pray over the thousands of prayer requests and pledge slips received during a TBN Praise-a-Thon.

A GLOBAL OUTREACH TO CHILDREN

In the 1980s Jan Crouch visited Haiti and later founded Smile of a Child. What began as a humanitarian Christian feeding mission and toy drive has become a global outreach mission. Today, Smile of a Child touches the lives of tens of thousands of needy children throughout the world and is building hospitals in Haiti and Costa Rica.

SMILE OF A CHILD
(right) Jan's ministry to children started in TBN's early days. Through her Smile of a Child outreach, she has distributed millions of toys to needy children worldwide and is building hospitals in Haiti and Costa Rica.

LITTLE ONES
(left) Jan doing what she loves best: ministering to children in Port-au-Prince, Haiti.
(right) Laurie Crouch and Jan visit a children's feeling center in Haiti. Jan's Smile of a Child foundation helps provide food for the center.
(below, left) Jan hosts Haitian prime minister Gerard Latortue and his staff and cabinet members at TBN's Florida station.

PRAYERFUL RESPONSE
(left) America and the world were rocked by the terrorist attacks of 9/11. Paul called the worldwide TBN family to prayer during a somber Praise the Lord program. (bottom) Paul calls the TBN family to prayer for U.S. and coalition forces stationed around the world.

NEW TERRITORY

*(clockwise from top) Paul talks with U.S. troops
on the parade grounds in front of Saddam
Hussein's former Arch of Triumph, a 150-foot
replica of his hands holding crossed swords.
While in Baghdad, Paul purchased a satellite dish from
a street vendor. Pastors and other Christian leaders in
Iraq received satellite dishes donated to them by TBN.
Paul and Matt Crouch in Baghdad on the parade
grounds in front of the former Arch of Triumph.*

TBN now reaches every major continent through fifty-three satellites and more than twelve thousand television stations and cable affiliates worldwide. The vision born to Paul and Jan Crouch in a small studio in 1973 is still being fulfilled, to the glory of God.

"TBN's goal is to inspire people, engage their minds, and encourage their spirit through contemporary and positive programming that speaks to people from all walks of life."

—*Paul Crouch Sr.*

TO ALL THE WORLD
(top to bottom) In 2005, Paul met Israeli prime minister Ariel Sharon in Jerusalem. In 2000, Paul traveled to Beijing, China, where he met with Mr. Zhao Qizheng, the Chinese minister of information. (below) Paul speaks to the audience attending a Benny Hinn service in Lagos, Nigeria. When he asked how many could watch TBN on their home television sets, nearly every hand was raised.

CONTENTS

NEW FAITH
A water baptism at Newton Lake in Pennsylvania in the 1920s. On the right, wearing a suit, is J.R. Flower, a longtime leader in the Assemblies of God.

T HE MOST SIGNIFICANT SPIRITUAL EVENT OF THE PAST CENTURY—AND ONE OF THE MOST IMPORTANT RELIGIOUS EVENTS OF ALL TIME—BEGAN APRIL 14, 1906, IN A DILAPIDATED BUILDING AT 312 AZUSA STREET IN DOWNTOWN LOS ANGELES. THE REVIVAL THERE, LED BY A HALF-BLIND AFRICAN AMERICAN PREACHER FROM HOUSTON, WAS HAILED BY SOME AS THE RENEWAL OF PENTECOST AND DERIDED BY OTHERS AS "WEIRD BABEL," BUT WITHIN A FEW YEARS IT HAD SWEPT THE GLOBE, TOUCHING MILLIONS, SPAWNING NEW DENOMINATIONS AND MINISTRIES, AND TRANSFORMING CHRISTENDOM FOREVER.

Today, the Pentecostal-Charismatic movement that sprang from the unlikely prayer meeting at Azusa Street counts 600 million followers worldwide and growing. It is "Christianity's fastest growing branch" and continues to shape the church at large. According to a 1998 *Newsweek* poll, nearly half of all Christians in the United States say they have "personally experienced the Holy Spirit," and three-quarters of all evangelical Protestants make the same claim.[1] These pages tell the story of the revival that began at Azusa Street and how in a single century this spiritual brushfire has revolutionized the Christian experience.

WILLIAM SEYMOUR AND THE AZUSA STREET REVIVAL

"Such a hunger to have more of God was in my heart," Seymour later said, "that I prayed for five hours a day for two and a half years."

All photos courtesy of Flower Pentecostal Heritage Center

William Seymour, c. 1912.

MANY LEADERS EMERGED FROM THE AZUSA STREET REVIVAL, BUT THE MOST SIGNIFICANT PERSON ASSOCIATED WITH THE REVIVAL ITSELF WAS THE SON OF FORMER SLAVES, WILLIAM JOSEPH SEYMOUR. SEYMOUR WAS BORN IN 1870 IN CENTERVILLE, LOUISIANA, AND WAS RAISED IN THE LOCAL BAPTIST CHURCH. AS A BOY HE WAS SPIRITUALLY INCLINED AND HAD MYSTICAL EXPERIENCES, DREAMS AND VISIONS. AS AN ADULT, SMALLPOX LEFT HIM BLIND IN HIS LEFT EYE. TO THOSE WHO KNEW HIM, SEYMOUR WAS A MAN OF UNCOMMON SPIRITUAL HUNGER.

In 1895, when he was twenty-five, Seymour moved to Indianapolis and worked as a waiter in a fashionable restaurant, but in 1900 he moved to Cincinnati and discovered holiness teachings through the Church of God (Anderson, Indiana), known then as the "Evening Light Saints." They taught that a second work of grace called *sanctification* would eradicate the power of "inbred sin" in a believer's life, a doctrine preached by John Wesley in the eighteenth century. Seymour embraced this teaching and moved to Houston in 1903. There he began attending a black Holiness church pastored by Lucy Farrow, the niece of the famous abolitionist Frederick Douglass. "Such a hunger to have more of God was in my heart," Seymour later said, "that I prayed for five hours a day for two and a half years."

Those prayers would soon show great effect.

LUCY FARROW

Lucy Farrow was born in slavery in Norfolk, Virginia, and distinguished herself as a teacher, preacher, and missionary in early Pentecostalism. Many received the baptism in the Holy Spirit through the laying on of her hands. She departed Los Angeles in August 1906 on her way to Liberia, West Africa, from which her ancestors had been brought to America. Stopping in Houston, she was invited by Charles Parham to preach at his camp meeting in progress. As she preached and shared about the revival in Los Angeles, the power of God fell, and many were baptized in the Holy Spirit. One of the participants, Howard Goss, who became a prominent leader in the movement, said she demonstrated "an unusual power to lay hands on people for the reception of the Holy Spirit."

That a black woman preached to a white audience in the segregated South in 1906 demonstrates the power of the Azusa Street revival to break color barriers, although at times temporarily. After returning to Los Angeles from Liberia, West Africa, in fall 1907, Farrow spent the remainder of her life in a small "faith cottage" behind the Azusa Street Mission where she ministered to many who sought her prayers.

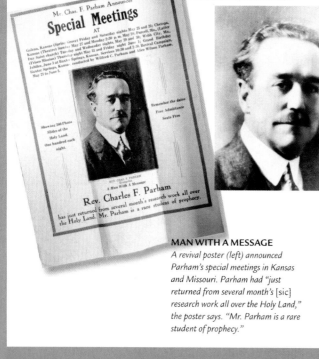

MAN WITH A MESSAGE
A revival poster (left) announced Parham's special meetings in Kansas and Missouri. Parham had "just returned from several month's [sic] research work all over the Holy Land," the poster says. "Mr. Parham is a rare student of prophecy."

SPREADING THE WORD
Charles Parham (right) with song leader Fred Campbell at Perryton, Texas, in the 1920s.

STONE'S FOLLY
Site of Charles Parham's Bethel Bible College in Topeka, Kansas (c. 1901). There, Parham and the students experienced a dramatic outpouring of the Holy Spirit during which virtually everyone present spoke in tongues.

SEYMOUR MEETS CHARLES PARHAM

In summer 1905, Charles F. Parham, a white Holiness preacher, came to Houston and conducted a citywide crusade in Bryan Hall. Parham had begun preaching a controversial third blessing after sanctification, which he called *the baptism in the Holy Spirit*. He and the students at his Bethel Bible College in Topeka had arrived at this doctrine during the closing days of 1900 and had experienced a dramatic outpouring of the Holy Spirit during which virtually everyone present spoke in tongues. Parham considered this to be a sign of the last days—God's way of restoring to the church apostolic faith of the New Testament. It also confirmed to him that the baptism in the Holy Spirit would be accompanied, or "evidenced," by speaking in tongues.

Parham found many receptive souls in Houston, including Seymour's friend Lucy Farrow, who heartily welcomed his message. Farrow developed such a friendship with the Parhams that they invited her to serve as a governess to their children when they returned to their home in Baxter Springs. She turned the pastorate of her congregation over to Seymour and, while staying

REVIVAL IN HOUSTON
In summer 1905, Parham (seated in the center of the third row) conducted a citywide crusade in Houston's Bryan Hall. Many there embraced his teaching about the baptism in the Holy Spirit.

in the Parham home in Baxter Springs, Kansas, experienced her own Spirit baptism and spoke in tongues.

In fall 1905 Farrow returned with the Parhams to Houston for another crusade at Bryan Hall. Parham was now planning to open a Bible school on January 1, 1906, and Farrow encouraged Seymour to enroll. Seymour, still driven by a deep desire for God, immediately applied for admission, but his application posed a problem because of Jim Crow laws and customs that mandated racial segregation. Parham skirted these rules by allowing Seymour to sit in an adjoining room and listen to classes

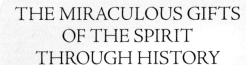

THE MIRACULOUS GIFTS OF THE SPIRIT THROUGH HISTORY

The work of the Holy Spirit and His gifts, including speaking in tongues, have occurred among Christians for the past two thousand years and were especially common during the first three centuries of the church's existence. Irenaeus, the well-known church father of the second century, spoke of healings, exorcisms, and even the raising of the dead in his time. He also said, "In like manner we do also hear many brethren in the church who possess prophetic gifts and who through the Spirit speak all kinds of languages." In the third century, the African church father Tertullian spoke of prophetic gifts and gifts of healing. He challenged the teachings of the heretic Marcion with logical arguments and then challenged him to prove his validity by demonstrating that miraculous gifts were operative in his life. He said, "Let him produce a psalm, a vision, a prayer—only let it be by the Spirit, in an ecstasy, that is in a rapture whenever an interpretation of tongues has occurred. *Now all these signs are forthcoming from my side without any difficulty.*"[2]

In the United States there were movings of the Holy Spirit as early as 1854 in New England among those who were known as "the Gift People." At Moorhead, Minnesota, in 1903, under the ministry of John Thompson, a minister of the Swedish Mission, the Holy Spirit was outpoured, and those receiving the Spirit spoke in new tongues.... The Holy Spirit was outpoured in the early days of [the Church of God] at the Shearer Schoolhouse in Cherokee County, North Carolina, and those who were baptized in the Holy Spirit spoke in tongues, others prophesied, and miracles of healing occurred.[3]

All photos courtesy of *Flower Pentecostal Heritage Center*

FROM *THE APOSTOLIC FAITH,* OCTOBER 1906 ISSUE

THE APOSTOLIC FAITH

"Earnestly contend for the faith which was once delivered unto the saints."—Jude 3.

Vol. 1, No. 2   Los Angeles, Cal., October, 1906.   Subscription Free

The Pentecostal Baptism Restored

The Promised Latter Rain Now Being Poured Out on God's Humble People.

Five years ago, God put it into [Charles Parham's] heart to go over to To-peka, Kansas, to educate missionaries to carry the Gospel. It was a faith school, and the Bible was the only textbook. The students had gathered there without tuition or board, God sending in the means to carry on the work. . . . Parham became convinced that there was no religious school that tallied up with the second chapter of Acts. Just before the first of January, 1901, the Bible School began to study the Word on the Baptism with the Holy Ghost to discover the Bible evidence of this baptism that they might obtain it.

The students kept up continual prayer in the praying tower. A company would go up and stay three hours, and then another company would go up and wait on God, praying that all the promises of the Word might be wrought out in their lives.

On New Year's night, Miss Agnes N. Oz-man was convinced of the need of a personal Pentecost. A few minutes before midnight, she desired hands laid on her that she might receive the gift of the Holy Ghost. During prayer and invocation of hands, she was filled with the Holy Ghost and spoke with other tongues as the Spirit gave utterance.

This made all hungry. Scarcely eating or sleeping, the school with one accord waited on God. On the 3rd of January, 1901, suddenly twelve students were filled with the Holy Ghost and began to speak with other tongues, and when Bro. Parham returned and opened the door of the room where they were gathered, a wonderful sight met his eyes. The whole room was filled with a white sheen of light that could not be described, and twelve of the students were on their feet talking in different languages.

He said they seemed to pay no attention at all to him, and he knelt in one corner and said: "O God, what does this mean?" The Lord said: "Are you able to stand for the experience in the face of persecution and howling mobs?" He said: "Yes, Lord, if You will give me the experience, for the laborer must first be partaker of the fruits." Instantly the Lord took his vocal organs, and he was preaching the Word in another language.[4]

OUTPOURING
Agnes N. Ozman, pictured in 1937, was the first person to speak in tongues at Parham's Bethel Bible College in 1901.

through an open door. There, Seymour imbibed Parham's teaching of a baptism in the Holy Spirit evidenced by speaking in tongues.

THE INVITATION TO LOS ANGELES

While attending classes and continuing to pastor his congregation in Houston, Seymour was invited to pastor a Los Angeles storefront Holiness mission whose parishioners were mostly black. This group had been expelled from the Second Baptist Church in Los Angeles because they had accepted the holiness teaching of a second blessing of sanctification. One of their members, Neeley Terry, had attended Seymour's church in Houston and was favorably impressed with him. She returned to Los Angeles, and her church promptly invited Seymour to pastor

RAISING THE BANNER
Parham (front) and followers outside a courthouse at Carthage, Missouri (c. 1905).

their congregation. After prayerfully considering the offer, Seymour accepted it and departed Houston in February 1906.

Seymour had not received the baptism in the Holy Spirit, but he was prepared to preach it without compromise. In his first service at the mission in Los Angeles he broached the subject of this so-called third blessing, but his audience equated the baptism in the Holy Spirit with their experience of sanctification and rejected the idea that tongues was necessary. When Seymour returned for the evening service, he found the door padlocked. The elders had decided he was preaching false doctrine. Less than a week after arriving in Los Angeles, Seymour was without a church.

EARLY FOLLOWERS
Parham and others in front of an Apostolic Faith mission, possibly at Joplin, Missouri (c. 1910). Their flag reads, "Our God, the Healer of His People."

"It was the divine call that brought me from Houston, Texas, to Los Angeles."

BURGEONING MOVEMENT
A camp meeting at Brunner Tabernacle in Houston, Texas (c. 1906). Parham is in the second row by the post and Howard Goss is in the front row on the far right. The sign reads, "Apostolic faith. Our faith is built on experiential salvation."

In His Own Words
WILLIAM SEYMOUR'S CALL TO LOS ANGELES

It was the divine call that brought me from Houston, Texas, to Los Angeles. The Lord put it in the heart of one of the saints in Los Angeles to write to me that she felt the Lord would have me come over here and do a work, and I came, for I felt it was the leading of the Lord. The Lord sent the means, and I came to take charge of a mission on Santa Fe Street, and one night they locked the door against me, and afterwards got Bro. Roberts, the president of the Holiness Association, to come down and settle the doctrine of the Baptism with the Holy Ghost, that it was simply sanctification. He came down and a good many holiness preachers with him, and they stated that sanctification was the baptism with the Holy Ghost. But yet they did not have the evidence at the second chapter of Acts, for when the disciples were all filled with the Holy Ghost, they spoke in tongues as the Spirit gave utterance. After the president heard me speak of what the true baptism of the Holy Ghost was, he said he wanted it too, and told me that when I had received it to let him know. So I received it and let him know. The beginning of the Pentecost started in a cottage prayer meeting at 214 Bonnie Brae. [5]

REVIVAL BREAKS FORTH

Some members of the mission took compassion on Seymour and invited him to stay in the homes of Edward Lee and then Richard Asberry, who lived at 214 Bonnie Brae Street. Seymour, driven by an almost overwhelming hunger for the power of the Holy Spirit, spent nearly all his time in prayer. He later said:

> I got to Los Angeles, and there the hunger [to have more of God] was not less but more. I prayed, "God, what can I do?" The Spirit said, "Pray more." "But Lord, I am praying five hours a day now." I increased my hours of prayer to seven, and prayed on....I prayed to God to give what Parham preached, the real Holy Ghost and fire with tongues with love and power of God like the apostles had.[6]

Because of Seymour's devotion to prayer, the Asberrys opened their home to evening prayer meetings. Seymour told the group about Lucy Farrow, who had introduced him to the idea of the baptism in the Holy Spirit. They were so anxious to meet her that they took up an offering for her train fare and invited her to come.

A few days later Edward Lee returned home after work to find Farrow just arrived from Houston. He was so hungry for the baptism in the Holy Spirit that after a brief introduction he implored, "Sister, if you will lay your hands on me, I believe I will get my baptism right now." She replied, "I cannot do it unless the Lord says so." Later, while eating dinner, Farrow rose from her seat, walked over to Lee, and said, "The Lord tells me to lay my hands on you for the Holy Ghost." She laid her hands on Lee, who immediately fell out of his chair and, while lying on the floor, began speaking in tongues.[7]

BEGINNINGS
At left, William J. Seymour with wife, Jennie Moore Seymour (1912). Below, the house on Bonnie Brae Street (1976) where Seymour's prayer meeting blossomed into the Azusa Street revival.

> *"As the people came in they would fall under God's power; and the whole city was stirred. They shouted there until the foundation of the house gave way."*

A NEW SONG
When revival broke out at the Bonne Brae Street home of Richard and Ruth Asberry (top) on April 9, 1906, Jennie Seymour, pictured in 1907, played the piano and sang in the Spirit, never having had a lesson.

REVIVAL COMES

Later that day the Lees and Farrow went to the Asberry home for the evening prayer meeting. Edward Lee walked through the door, lifted his hands, and broke out in tongues. Suddenly the power of God flooded the room, and virtually everyone present began speaking in tongues. One of those present was Jennie Moore, who later became Seymour's wife. She not only spoke in tongues but also went to the piano and played and sang in tongues, though she had never had a lesson.[8] An eyewitness to these events said:

> They shouted three days and three nights. It was the Easter season. The people came from everywhere. By the next morning there was no way of getting near the house. As the people came in they would fall under God's power; and the whole city was stirred. They shouted there until the foundation of the house gave way, but no one was hurt. During those three days there were many people who received their baptism. The sick were healed and sinners were saved just as they came in.[9]

Realizing that the Asberry home was too small to contain the crowds, Seymour and others looked for larger facilities and finally located an older building at 312 Azusa Street in downtown Los Angeles. This two-story structure, measuring 40 feet by 60 feet, had once been a Methodist Episcopal church, but more recently had been used as a stable and warehouse. They removed the debris and installed rough plank benches and a makeshift pulpit made from wooden shoeboxes. On April 14, 1906, they held their first meeting in the new facilities. So began the twentieth century's most momentous revival.

All photos courtesy of Flower Pentecostal Heritage Center

MOVE TO AZUSA

The prayer meeting at Bonnie Brae outgrew the Asberry home and was moved to a building on Azusa Street that had recently been used as a stable and warehouse (top, c. 1928). Participants in the Azusa Street Mission, pictured in 1907, included, seated (l-r), Sister Evans, Hiram W. Smith, William Seymour, Clara Lum; standing (l-r), an unidentified woman, Brother Evans (reportedly the first man to receive the baptism in the Holy Spirit at Azusa Street), Jennie Moore (later Mrs. William Seymour), Glenn A. Cook, Florence Crawford, an unidentified man, and Sister Prince. Florence Crawford's daughter Mildred is seated in Hiram Smith's lap.

A DAY AT THE AZUSA STREET REVIVAL

The services at Azusa were spontaneous, with no preannounced events, special choirs, singers, or well-known evangelists. There wasn't even a platform. Seymour, the recognized leader, spent much of his time behind the pulpit with his head inside the top shoebox, praying. A contemporary, John G. Lake, described Seymour like so:

> God had put such a hunger into that man's heart that when the fire of God came it glorified him. I do not believe any other man in modern times had a more wonderful deluge of God in his life than God gave to that dear fellow, and the glory and power of a real Pentecost swept the world. That black man preached to my congregation of ten thousand people when the glory and power of God was upon his spirit, and men shook and trembled and cried to God. God was in him.[10]

Prayer consumed the participants at Azusa Street. One participant said, "The whole place was steeped in prayer."[11] During meetings anyone was free to share a testimony or word of exhortation. One participant described a typical service.

> Someone might be speaking. Suddenly the Spirit would fall upon the congregation. God Himself would give the altar call. Men

---

The first issue of Seymour's newspaper, *The Apostolic Faith*, was published in September 1906. The lead story read:

PENTECOST HAS COME

Los Angeles Being Visited by a Revival of Bible Salvation and Pentecost as Recorded in the Books of Acts

The power of God now has this city agitated as never before. Pentecost has surely come and with it the Bible evidences are following, many being converted and sanctified and filled with the Holy Ghost, speaking in tongues as they did on the day of Pentecost. The scenes that are daily enacted in the building on Azusa street and at Missions and churches in other parts of the city are beyond description, and the real revival is only started, as God has been working with His children mostly, getting them through to Pentecost, and laying the foundation for a mighty wave of salvation among the unconverted.

The meetings are held in an old Methodist church that had been converted in part into a tenement house, leaving a large, unplastered, barn-like room on the ground floor. Here about a dozen congregated each day, holding meetings on Bonnie Brae in the evening. . . . In a short time God began to manifest His power and soon the building could not contain the people. Now the meetings continue all day and into the night and the fire is kindling all over the city and surrounding towns. Proud, well-dressed preachers come in to "investigate." Soon their high looks are replaced with wonder, then conviction comes, and very often you will find them in a short time wallowing on the dirty floor, asking God to forgive them and make them as little children.

It would be impossible to state how many have been converted, sanctified and filled with the Holy Ghost. They have been and are daily going out to all points of the compass to spread this wonderful gospel.[12]

VISITING AZUSA
S. D. Page (left) and F. M. Britton in front of the Azusa Street Mission in the 1920s. Britton became a leader of the Pentecostal Holiness denomination.

REVIVAL MAKES FRONT PAGE NEWS

On April 18, just four days after moving into the Azusa Street location, the revival made the front page of the Los Angeles Times.

THE HAPPENINGS AT AZUSA STREET

Weird Babel of Tongues

New Sect of Fanatics Is Breaking Loose

Wild Scene Last Night on Azusa Street

Gurgle of Wordless Talk by a Sister

Breathing strange utterances and mouthing a creed which it would seem no sane mortal could understand, the newest religious sect has started in Los Angeles. Meetings are held in a tumble-down shack on Azusa Street, near San Pedro Street, and devotees of the weird doctrine practice the most fanatical rites, preach the wildest theories and work themselves into a state of mad excitement in their peculiar zeal. Colored people and a sprinkling of whites compose the congregation, and night is made hideous in the neighborhood by the howlings of the worshippers who spend hours swaying forth and back in a nerve-racking [*sic*] attitude of prayer and supplication. They claim to have "the gift of tongues;" and to be able to comprehend the babel.

Such a startling claim has never yet been made by any company of fanatics, even in Los Angeles, the home of almost numberless creeds. Sacred tenets, reverently mentioned by the orthodox believer, are dealt with in a familiar, if not irreverent, manner by these latest religionists.

STONY OPTIC DEFIES

An old colored exhorter, blind in one eye, is the major-domo of the company. With his stony optic fixed on some luckless unbeliever, the old man yells his defiance and challenges an answer. Anathemas are heaped upon him who shall dare to gainsay the utterances of the preacher.

Clasped in his big fist the colored brother holds a miniature Bible from which he reads at intervals one or two words—never more. After an hour spent in exhortation the brethren present are invited to join in a "meeting of prayer, song and testimony." Then it is that pandemonium breaks loose, and the bounds of reason are passed by those who are "filled with the spirit," whatever that may be.

"You-oo-oogou-loo-loo come under the bloo-oo-oo boo-loo;" shouts an old colored "mammy;" in a frenzy of religious zeal. Swinging her arms wildly about her, she continues with the strangest harangue ever uttered. Few of her words are intelligible, and for the most part her testimony contains the most outrageous jumble of syllables, which are listened to with awe by the company.

LET TONGUES COME FORTH

One of the wildest of the meetings was held last night, and the highest pitch of excitement was reached by the gathering, which continued to "worship" until nearly midnight. The old exhorter urged the "sisters" to let the "tongues come forth" and the women gave themselves over to a riot of religious fervor. As a result a buxom dame was overcome with excitement and almost fainted.

Undismayed by the fearful attitude of the colored worshipper, another black women [*sic*] jumped to the floor and began a wild gesticulation, which ended in a gurgle of wordless prayers which were nothing less than shocking.

"She's speaking in unknown tongues;" announced the leader, in ah [*sic*] awed whisper, "keep on sister." The sister continued until it was necessary to assist her to a seat because of her bodily fatigue.

GOLD AMONG THEM

Among the "believers" is a man who claims to be a Jewish rabbi. He says his name is Gold, and claims to have held positions in some of the largest synagogues in the United States. He told the motley company last night that he is well known to the Jewish people of Los Angeles and San Francisco, and referred to prominent local citizens by name. Gold claims to have been miraculously healed and is a convert of the new sect.

Another speaker had a vision in which he saw the people of Los Angeles flocking in a mighty stream to perdition. He prophesied awful destruction to this city unless its citizens are brought to a belief in the tenets of the new faith.[13]

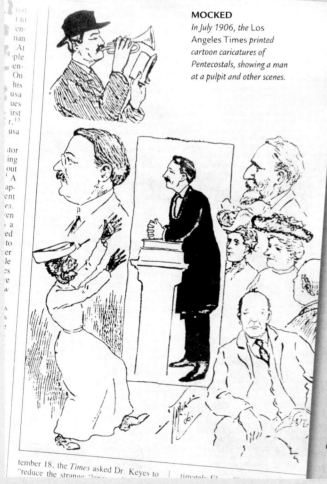

MOCKED
In July 1906, the Los Angeles Times *printed cartoon caricatures of Pentecostals, showing a man at a pulpit and other scenes.*

would fall all over the house, like the slain in battle, or rush for the altar *en masse* to seek God. Presumptuous men would sometimes come among us. Especially preachers who would try to spread themselves in self-opinionation. But their effort was short lived. Their minds would wander, their brains reel. Things would turn black before their eyes. They could not go on. We simply prayed. The Holy Ghost did the rest.[14]

The building was never empty of people at prayer, though services, such as they were, usually began spontaneously around mid-morning and continued until three or four the following morning. Dramatic spiritual manifestations captured the attention of the general public, but participants believed the most important feature of the revival was God's love in action. Frank Bartleman, a journalist and participant in the revival, described it as a return to the "first love" of the early church.

Divine love was wonderfully manifest in the meetings. They would not even allow an unkind word said against any of their opposers, or the churches. The message was the love of God. It was a sort of "first love" of the early church returned. The "baptism" as we received it in the beginning did not allow us to think, speak, or hear evil of any man. We knew the moment we had grieved the Spirit by an unkind thought or word. We seemed to live in a sea of pure divine love.[15]

GRACIOUS PENTECOSTAL SHOWERS CONTINUE TO FALL

The news has spread far and wide that Los Angeles is being visited with a "rushing mighty wind from heaven." The how and why of it is to be found in the very opposite of those conditions that are usually thought necessary for a big revival. No instruments of music are used, none are needed. No choir—but bands of angels have been heard by some in the spirit and there is a heavenly singing that is inspired by the Holy Ghost. No collections are taken. No bills have been posted to advertise the meetings. No church or organization is back of it. All who are in touch with God realize as soon as they enter the meetings that the Holy Ghost is the leader. One brother stated that even before his train entered the city, he felt the power of the revival.[16]

"We knew the moment we had grieved the Spirit by an unkind thought or word. We seemed to live in a sea of pure divine love."

AZUSA LEADERS
Azusa Street revival leaders (c. 1907) in front of the mission. Back row (l-r): Brother Adams, F. F. Bosworth, Tom Hezmalhalch. Seated: William J. Seymour, and John G. Lake.

FRANK BARTLEMAN

Frank Bartleman, an early Pentecostal evangelist and journalist, became the primary chronicler of the Azusa Street revival. Bartleman, known as something of a loner, participated in meetings at Azusa Street from 1906 to 1908 and wrote articles about the revival for various Christian publications. After departing Los Angeles, Bartleman preached throughout the United States and made an around-the-world ministry tour. He published his eyewitness of account of the Azusa Street revival in 1925 under the title *How Pentecost Came to Los Angeles*. The book is currently published under the title *Azusa Street*. Bartleman died in Burbank, California, in 1936.[17]

CROWDS FROM AROUND THE WORLD

At first the revival advanced slowly, with only 150 people receiving "the gift of the Holy Ghost and the Bible evidence" during the summer of 1906. But this changed in the fall as the revival gained momentum.[18] News of the revival began to raise wide interest, and soon the faithful and curious journeyed from far and near to experience it. Though passage was long and difficult, visitors poured in from across North America and from foreign soil, where word had spread among missionaries. The *Los Angeles Times'* negative coverage nevertheless caught people's attention. Bartleman sent his articles about the revival to Holiness publications throughout the country. Seymour founded a paper called *The Apostolic Faith*, which eventually reached a distribution of 40,000 copies. For practical purposes the prayer meeting was soon organized into a church called the Apostolic Faith Mission.

Many visitors had dramatic spiritual experiences unlike anything they had ever known before. Visitor Glenn A. Cook shared his testimony with *The Apostolic Faith* newspaper:

I could feel the power going through me like electric needles. The Spirit taught me that I must not resist the power but give way and become limp as a piece of cloth. When I did this, I fell under the power, and God began to mold me and teach me what it meant to be really surrendered to Him. I was laid out under the power five times before Pentecost really came. Each time I would come out from under the power, I would feel so sweet and clean, as though I had been run through a washing machine....My arms began to tremble, and soon I was shaken violently by a great power, and it seemed as though a large pipe was fitted over my neck, my head apparently being off....About thirty hours afterwards, while sitting in the meeting on Azusa Street, I felt my throat and tongue begin to move, without any effort on my part. Soon I began to stutter and then out came a distinct language which I could hardly restrain. I talked and laughed with joy far into the night.[19]

Another visitor, G. W. Batman wrote, "I received the baptism with the Holy Ghost and

REVIVAL'S JOURNALIST
Frank Bartleman (left, c. 1894) as a young man, and pictured at 8th and Maple Street Pentecostal Assembly in Los Angeles, where he ministered.

fire and now I feel the presence of the Holy Ghost, not only in my heart but in my lungs, my hands, my arms and all through my body and at times I am shaken like a locomotive steamed up and prepared for a long journey."[20]

Countless thousands had similar deeply personal experiences, spoke in tongues, wept, and went home with fresh zeal and empowerment to spread the gospel.

CHRIST AT THE CENTER OF AZUSA STREET

Though Azusa Street quickly became known for the manifestations of the Holy Spirit, like miraculous gifts and speaking in tongues, the participants kept their attention squarely on Jesus. Frank Bartleman expressed the general desire that Jesus should not be "lost in the temple" by the exaltation of the Holy Ghost and of the gifts of the Spirit. "I endeavored to keep Him as the central theme and figure before the people," Bartleman said. "The Holy Ghost never draws attention from Christ to Himself, but rather reveals Christ in a fuller way." When once asked by a certain woman to pray that she might speak in tongues, Seymour kindly exhorted, "Now, look here, Sister Sadie, don't you ever go looking for tongues. Seek Jesus for Himself. Seek the Lord. He's the One."

In Their Own Words . . .

The Holy Spirit fell upon me and filled me literally, as it seemed to lift me up, for indeed, I was in the air in an instant, shouting, 'Praise God,' and instantly I began to speak in another language. I could not have been more surprised if at the same moment someone had handed me a million dollars.[21]

—Account from a Baptist pastor visiting the Azusa Street revival

❖

By the time the chorus ended, the power of God was so heavy upon me. I could scarcely open my mouth, and every fibre of my being was trembling. Yet my feet felt glued to the floor and my knees stiff, so I could not sit down. I only got out a few broken sentences that I remember. (I never fainted in my life and was never unconscious, but God certainly took me out of myself.) He showed me things which there are not words enough in the English language to express . . . I was under the power the remainder of the meeting, and for three days was as one drunken . . . Since then, such waves of power roll over me from time to time. I can scarcely keep my feet, and I am sure if my old friends in California could see me, they would think I was indeed insane.[22]

—Testimony of Myrtle K. Shideler

❖

Scenes transpiring here [on Azusa Street] are what Los Angeles churches have been praying for for years. I have been a Methodist for twenty-five years. I was leader of the praying band for the First Methodist Church. We prayed that Pentecost might come to the city of Los Angeles. We wanted it to start in the First Methodist Church, but God did not start it there. I bless God that it did not start in any church in this city, but in a barn, so that we might all come and take part in it. If it had started in a fine church, the poor colored people and Spanish people would not have got it, but praise God it started here.[23]

—Testimony of a leading Methodist layman of Los Angeles

TENT MEETING
John G. Lake and others on the platform of a revival meeting in Milwaukee, Wisconsin.

HIGHWAYS AND BYWAYS

*An evangelistic team and
house trailer at Hickory Grove,
Oklahoma, in 1912.*

DENOMINATIONS SWEPT INTO REVIVAL

Photo courtesy of IPHC

I N NOVEMBER 1906, GASTON B. CASHWELL, AN EVAN-
GELIST WITH THE PENTECOSTAL HOLINESS CHURCH
OF NORTH CAROLINA, ARRIVED AT THE AZUSA STREET
MISSION. HE HAD READ OF THE REVIVAL IN A PUBLICATION
CALLED THE *WAY OF FAITH* AND HAD COME TO SEE FOR HIM-
SELF IF AZUSA STREET WAS THE REVIVAL HE AND OTHERS
HAD BEEN PRAYING FOR. SO DESPERATE WAS CASHWELL FOR
A DEEPER WALK WITH GOD THAT HE BORROWED MONEY FOR
A ONE-WAY TRAIN TICKET AND, WEARING HIS ONLY SUIT,
CAME TO LOS ANGELES.

REVIVAL SPREADS EAST
G. B. Cashwell (above) visited the Azusa Street revival, then led a powerful revival in North Carolina that transformed many lives and several denominations in the South and East.

During Cashwell's first service at the Azusa Street Mission, a young black man laid his hands on him and prayed that he might receive the "baptism." Such close racial interaction rankled Cashwell, and he left the meeting offended and disappointed. Back in his hotel

ON THE EAST COAST, "ANOTHER AZUSA STREET"

After returning home to Dunn, North Carolina, Cashwell preached in the local Holiness church and told of his experience in Los Angeles. Interest ran so high that he

Thousands crowded into the warehouse, and scores were baptized in the Holy Spirit and spoke in tongues.

room he "suffered a crucifixion" as God dealt severely with him about his racial prejudice. He later said that God gave him a love for blacks and a renewed hunger to be baptized in the Holy Spirit. He returned to the mission the next night and asked Seymour and several young black people to lay their hands on him and pray that he might receive the baptism in the Holy Spirit. Cashwell received his Spirit baptism and, according to his own account, spoke in English, German, and French.[24] Seymour received an offering for him and presented him with a new suit and enough money for his return fare to North Carolina.

rented a three-story tobacco warehouse and conducted a month-long Pentecostal revival. Thousands crowded into the warehouse, and scores were baptized in the Holy Spirit and spoke in tongues. People came from all over the Southeast, and the revival became for the East Coast "another Azusa Street."[25]

Among the attendees were pastors and leaders from the four largest Holiness groups in the area: the Pentecostal Holiness churches, the Fire-Baptized Holiness churches, Holiness Free-Will Baptist churches, and Tabernacle Pentecostal churches. Many of these pastors were baptized in the Holy Spirit and spoke

REVIVAL IN ZION CITY, ILLINOIS

Zion City, Illinois, forty miles north of Chicago on Lake Michigan, was founded as a Christian city by well-known healing revivalist John Alexander Dowie. Many devout Christians relocated to Zion from across the United States and from other nations. Their dream of living in a Christian utopia was shattered, however, when the city was plunged into bankruptcy and Dowie was ousted from leadership. Into this tumultuous atmosphere Charles Parham arrived in 1906 with his message of a baptism in the Holy Spirit evidenced by speaking in tongues. Wilbur Voliva, who had just wrested control of the city from Dowie, sought to block Parham's ministry in Zion by renting every auditorium in the city. Parham responded by conducting meetings in some of the largest homes, including the home of F. F. Bosworth.

A Pentecostal revival erupted, and people crowded into the homes and overflowed onto the lawns. The *Daily Sun* of Waukegan, Illinois, reported that thousands attended the meetings. The work of the Holy Spirit was deep and powerful, according to eyewitness accounts. Many prominent leaders came out of the Zion revival including John G. Lake, F. F. Bosworth, and approximately five hundred other missionaries and ministers.[26]

MAKING NEWS

A Los Angeles newspaper reported December 4, 1906, that a Nebraska woman had received the "gift of tongues."

in tongues. Almost overnight, these pastors and their churches became full-fledged participants in the Pentecostal revival. The Pentecostal Holiness Church later merged with the Fire-Baptized Holiness Church and the new group retained the name Pentecostal Holiness Church. This group then merged with the Tabernacle Pentecostal Church to form what is today known as the International Pentecostal Holiness Church, one of the oldest and largest Pentecostal denominations.

ZION CITY'S REVIVAL

After Zion City collapsed financially and spiritually under the leadership of John Alexander Dowie, shown (right) wearing high priestly robes as the self-proclaimed first apostle in the Christian Catholic Apostolic Church (1904), the community experienced Pentecostal revival in 1906 under Charles Parham. Pictured above (c. 1909) are participants in that revival.

THE CHURCH OF GOD IN CHRIST

Charles H. Mason and the Church of God in Christ (COGIC) were swept into the Pentecostal revival when Mason visited the Azusa Street Mission during the fall of 1906. Mason and Charles Price Jones had founded the Church of God in Christ in 1897 after being ostracized by their Baptist colleagues when they embraced the Wesleyan-Holiness doctrine of sanctification. By 1906 the COGIC had grown into a small network of churches in the South and Southwest.

Mason spent five weeks in Los Angeles, mostly at the Azusa Street Mission praying and seeking the baptism in the Holy Spirit. One day while sitting in the mission, someone said, "Let us sing." Mason stood to his feet and began to sing, "He Brought Me Out of the Miry Clay." He later described what happened.

"The Spirit came upon the saints and upon me. Then I gave up for the Lord to have His way within me. So there came a wave of Glory into me and all of my being was filled with the Glory of the Lord. So when He had gotten me straight on my feet, there came a light which enveloped my entire being above the brightness of the sun. When I opened my mouth to say Glory, a flame touched my tongue which ran down me. My language changed and no word could I speak in my own tongue. Oh! I was filled with the Glory of the Lord. My soul was then satisfied."[27]

When he returned home to Memphis and shared his experience with Jones and their congregation, Mason encountered much opposition. After several days of intense debate, he and Jones separated and the church split. Those who followed Mason reorganized their group and retained the name of Church of God in Christ. The Church of God in Christ, whose constituency is primarily African American, would become the largest Pentecostal denomination in America with a membership estimated at 5.5 million.

FOUNDER

Charles H. Mason cofounded the Church of God in Christ in 1897 and embraced the Pentecostal message in 1906 after visiting the Azusa Street revival. Below, Mason is pictured sitting (front, center) at a COGIC meeting in Memphis, Tennessee, in 1932.

TONGUES AS REAL LANGUAGES

Albert Norton, missionary to India when the Holy Spirit was poured out in 1906, described his amazement at hearing illiterate Indians speaking in fluent English when they were baptized in the Holy Spirit. The following incident occurred in a home for girls operated by Pandita Ramabai, who has been called the "Mother of the Pentecostal Movement" in India.

One week ago I visited the Mukti Mission. Miss Abrams asked me if I would like to go into a room where about twenty girls were praying. After entering, I knelt with closed eyes by a table on one side. Presently I heard someone praying near me in very distinct English. Among the petitions were, "O Lord, open the mouth; O Lord, open the heart; Oh, the blood of Jesus, the blood of Jesus!" I was struck with such astonishment, as I knew there was no one in the room who could speak English, besides Miss Abrams. I opened my eyes and within three feet of me, on her knees with closed eyes and raised hands was a woman I had baptized at Kedgaon in 1899, and whom my wife and I had known intimately since. Her mother tongue was Marathi and she could speak a little Hindustani. But when I heard her speak English idiomatically, distinctly and fluently, I was impressed as I should have been had I seen one, whom I knew to be dead, raised to life. A few other illiterate Marathi women and girls were speaking in English and some were speaking in other languages which none at Kedgaon understood.[28]

PENTECOST IN INDIA
Pandita Ramabai (center), known as the "Mother of the Pentecostal Movement" in India, with a group of babies at her Mukti Mission.

THE MISSIONS EMPHASIS

Seymour and the others at the Azusa Street revival believed God was pouring out His Spirit to empower Christians to evangelize the world just before the return of Christ to the earth. So strongly did this vision permeate their thinking that in the early days they believed speaking in tongues was missionary tongues by which people would evangelize the heathen. Although they eventually backed away from this misconception, they held firmly to their belief that God was pouring out His Spirit for the sake of world evangelism.

This vision impelled many missionaries to depart from the revival for various parts of the world. Lucy Farrow went to Africa; Alfred and Lillian Garr to India; Samuel and Adrella Mead to Africa; Ansel and Etta Post to Egypt; and Louise Condit and Lucy Leatherman to Jerusalem. Each went in faith, trusting God for provision and relying on the Holy Spirit to lead them in their endeavors.

GOING FORTH
Lillian Garr (right), an early Pentecostal missionary to India, with Lillian Denny.

THE MISSIONARY CALL

Many future leaders were called to missions and ministry in the wake of Azusa Street.

MARIE BURGESS BROWN (1880-1971), who became a successful pastor in the Assemblies of God, was baptized in the Holy Spirit in the home of F. F. Bosworth in Zion City. She said:

> I remember October 18, 1906, when the Lord baptized me in the Holy Spirit. For six hours He moved upon me in intercessory prayer for various mission fields. First He took me to China. I saw high stone walls and from beyond them heard the Chinese crying for help. Then the Lord took me to India. There I saw the people of different castes, and I wondered and wept. But even

PASTOR IN NEW YORK CITY
Marie Burgess Brown, pictured in 1960, was baptized in the Holy Spirit in the home of F. F. Bosworth at Zion City and founded Glad Tidings Tabernacle in New York City. Glad Tidings became one of the most prominent Pentecostal churches in the nation.

> as I wept for India's lost, the Lord showed me the continent of Africa. I preached to those people and they were especially responsive. Then in a vision I went to Japan. There I entered an orphanage, and one by one the children came to me.[29]

Brown assumed that God was calling her to one of these nations as a missionary. After this experience, however, she went to New York City and founded Glad Tidings Tabernacle, which became one of the most prominent Pentecostal churches in the nation. Although she never personally visited any of those nations, the church she pastored for more than sixty years, until her death in 1971, eventually sent missionaries to every nation she had seen in the vision.

REVIVAL IN CHINA

WILLIAM SIMPSON (1869–1961), Christian and Missionary Alliance missionary to China, was baptized in the Holy Spirit in 1912. Shortly thereafter he returned to the United States and affiliated with the newly formed Assemblies of God. China, however, was still much on his heart, and, at a camp meeting in 1918, an amazing miracle occurred that thrust him back to China. He said:

> In a camp meeting the Spirit spoke just as directly to me as He had spoken long ago to Paul: It was in Chinese through a sister who knew not one word of Chinese, and told me to go back to Taochow on the Tibetan border. So I was sent forth by the Holy Spirit, sailing again on February 4, 1918. The

WILLIAM SIMPSON
Missionary William Simpson (pictured left in 1918, and above c. 1934 with his family) participated in a powerful outpouring of the Spirit in China.

> Lord opened the way until we reached the border, and as soon as we arrived on that mission field the Spirit of God was poured out.... We received letters inviting us here and there, and wherever we went the Spirit was poured out in Pentecostal power.[30]

A WORLDWIDE PHENOMENON

The revival at Azusa Street continued unabated for about three years (1906–1909) and was a fountainhead of Pentecost for the entire world. For a time, the revival produced amazing racial harmony in a country divided by racist laws and customs. People of many races met there, and an amazing unity prevailed. Blacks, whites, Mexican Americans, and many others knelt together in prayer and waited for their personal Pentecost. Bartleman said, "The color line was washed away in the blood."[31]

The original Azusa board of directors, which governed the affairs of the mission and issued ministerial credentials, consisted of seven women and five men. Five of the women were white and two were black. Of the five men, four were white and one, Seymour, was black.

The revival also brought women into positions of leadership they had not achieved in broader society. Women had not yet won the right to vote in U.S. elections and were excluded by most churches from any real leadership positions. Yet women comprised a majority on the Azusa Street Mission's governing board, and many powerful women evangelists, pastors, and missionaries went forth from the revival. Lucy Farrow took her evangelistic endeavors to Los Angeles, Texas, Virginia, New York, and Liberia, West Africa. Florence Crawford served on the governing board of the Azusa Street Mission and later founded the Apostolic Mission of Portland, Oregon. She served as pastor and overseer of

MISSION LEADER
Florence L. Crawford with son Raymond and daughter Mildred (c. 1910s).

MOTHER COTTON
Azusa Street revival participant and church planter Emma L. Cotton with husband Henry (c. 1939).

this network of churches until her death in 1936. Emma "Mother" Cotton founded and pastored several churches on the West Coast. These and many other women believed their experience of the Spirit fulfilled Joel's prophecy that was quoted by Peter on the Day of Pentecost.

> And it shall come to pass in the last days, says God, that I will pour out of My Spirit on all flesh; your sons and your daughters shall prophesy.…And on My menservants and on My maidservants I will pour out My Spirit in those days; and they will prophesy.
> —Acts 2:17, NKJV

Their experience at Azusa Street gave them a strong vision for egalitarian ministry in the last days.

Ultimately, however, doctrinal and racial strife drove participants apart. Many white people left to begin their own churches and missions. By 1914, the Azusa Street Mission

> For a time, the revival produced amazing racial harmony. People of many races met there, and an amazing unity prevailed.

had become a small, local, black congregation.

Seymour continued as the senior pastor until his death on September 28, 1922, in Los Angeles. His wife, the former Jennie Moore, continued as pastor for several years until her health failed. The mission was torn down in 1931 and the property made into a parking lot. Azusa Street's days as a catalyst for worldwide revival were over, but the influence of the revival had just begun.

WASHED ANEW
*The baptism of Hannah
Wiley in a river near Joplin,
Missouri (c. 1910).*

REVIVAL SPREADS AND DIVERSIFIES

AS PILGRIMS TO AZUSA STREET DEPARTED WITH THE LOVE AND POWER OF GOD BURN-ING IN THEIR HEARTS, THE PENTECOSTAL REVIVAL SPREAD AS FAST AS WORD OF MOUTH COULD CARRY IT. PENTECOSTAL CHURCHES SPRUNG UP THROUGHOUT THE COUNTRY, OFTEN IN THE FORM OF SMALL STOREFRONT MISSIONS. OTHER CHURCHES BECAME IN-FLUENTIAL CENTERS OF REVIVAL AND HELPED SPREAD THE FIRE OF PENTECOST THROUGHOUT THE NATION AND THE WORLD. ONE OF THESE CENTERS WAS THE NORTH AVENUE MISSION IN CHICAGO WHOSE PASTOR, WILLIAM DURHAM, VISITED THE AZUSA STREET REVIVAL IN 1907.

WILLIAM DURHAM AND REVIVAL IN CHICAGO

Durham had joined a Baptist church in Kentucky in 1891 and was converted seven years later in Minnesota where he had a vision of the crucified Christ. He devoted himself completely to God and three years later, in 1901, became the pastor of the North Avenue Mission in Chicago. Upon hearing of the Azusa Street revival, he journeyed there in March 1907 and was baptized in the Holy Spirit and spoke in tongues. At the same

time, Seymour prophesied to him that wherever he preached, the Holy Spirit would fall upon the people.[32]

Durham returned to Chicago with his new experience and message, and as he preached, a powerful revival broke forth in the North Avenue Mission.

DURHAM'S MINISTRY
William H. Durham's first camp meeting (above, c. 1909). Durham is standing in center with his hand raised. At left, Durham with Harry Van Loon (left) in the 1910s.

TESTIMONY
The Pentecostal Testimony announced William H. Durham's death on its cover in 1912.

APOSTOLIC FAITH

In His Own Words

Baptism Restored

William H. Durham recorded his testimony in the sixth issue of *The Apostolic Faith* (February–March 1907), where he wrote:

> On Friday evening, March 1, His mighty power came over me, until I jerked and quaked under it for about three hours. It was strange and wonderful and yet glorious. He worked my whole body, one section at a time, first my arms, then my limbs, then my body, then my head, then my face, then my chin, and finally at 1 a.m. Saturday, March 2, after being under the power for three hours, He finished the work on my vocal organs, and spoke through me in unknown tongues.

In his periodical the *Pentecostal Testimony*, Durham reported that, "It was nothing to hear people at all hours of the night speaking in tongues and singing in the Spirit."[33] Participants saw a thick haze, like blue smoke, resting upon the mission at times. They said that when this blue haze was present, those entering the mission would fall down in the aisles.[34]

As news of this revival spread, the North Avenue Mission became another important center for Pentecostalism. A. H. Argue of Winnipeg, who became a Pentecostal leader in Canada, received his baptism in the Spirit there, as did E. N. Bell of Texas, who became one of the founders of the Assemblies of God and its first general superintendent.

Aimee Semple McPherson, who later founded the Church of the Foursquare Gospel and became one of America's most famous preachers, visited the revival at North Avenue Mission in 1910 and testified that she was instantly healed of a broken foot during the meeting. She and husband Robert Semple were ordained by Durham and worked with him in evangelistic crusades.

A. H. ARGUE, 1917

E. N. BELL, C. 1920

Seymour and the earliest Pentecostals adopted the name "the Apostolic Faith" for their movement because they believed that God was restoring to the entire church the apostolic faith of the New Testament with accompanying gifts and graces. But eventually those going out from the Los Angeles revival stopped using the term "Apostolic Faith" and instead called themselves "Pentecostals" to put themselves in the same tradition as the disciples on the Day of Pentecost (Acts 2).

DOCTRINAL CONTROVERSY

In addition to being a catalyst for revival, Durham instigated one of the first major doctrinal controversies of the fledgling movement. Being from a Baptist background, Durham believed sanctification occurred at conversion and was expressed by a growth in grace toward maturity. For him, the baptism in the Holy Spirit was a second blessing. He could not accept the doctrine taught by Seymour and other early Pentecostals of a definite, second work of grace called *sanctification* with the baptism in the Holy Spirit being a third blessing. When he began to openly oppose the Wesleyan-Holiness doctrine of *sanctification*, strife erupted throughout the movement.

Although Durham's teaching on sanctification, which he called "The Finished Work," provoked much dissension throughout the revival, it also had a positive effect. Many hungry souls from non-Wesleyan backgrounds were drawn to Durham's message, and it made it easier for them to embrace the revival. Multitudes reared in Baptistic/Reformed churches began embracing the Pentecostal message, further accelerating the movement's astonishing growth. The revival was proving adaptable at drawing people from differing and even opposing theological camps.

THE CHURCH OF GOD

In the meantime another Holiness denomination based in Cleveland, Tennessee, was drawn into the Pentecostal movement through the ministry of G. B. Cashwell, who became known as "the Apostle of Pentecost to the South." Cashwell visited Cleveland, Tennessee, in 1908 and preached in the local Church of God. This small network of Holiness churches had experienced speaking in tongues at one of their camp meetings in 1898 but had never made tongues an official doctrine of their church. On Sunday, January 12, 1908, A. J. Tomlinson, the general overseer of this denomination, sat on the platform as Cashwell preached on the baptism in the Holy Spirit. As Cashwell spoke, Tomlinson suddenly fell from his chair onto the floor and began speaking in tongues. According to his own testimony, he spoke in ten different languages while lying on the floor. The Church of God instantly became part of the Pentecostal movement and eventually grew to four million adherents worldwide. The denomination sponsored Lee University and the Church of God School of Theology, both in Cleveland, and began operating college-level educational institutions in South Africa, Indonesia, Korea, Puerto Rico, Germany, Panama, Mexico, Argentina, and the Philippines.

PENTECOSTAL Camp Meeting

To be held at Martinsville, Indiana During the Month of August, 1915

DIVINE SHIFT
A. J. Tomlinson, pictured here as a young man, was the general overseer of the Church of God when the denomination embraced the Pentecostal message.

THE ASSEMBLIES OF GOD

As hundreds of independent Pentecostal churches and missions sprouted up throughout the country, problems and confusion arose along with them. Some churches used the same names without realizing it, most were not legally incorporated, and many independent churches naïvely welcomed anyone claiming to be a Pentecostal preacher. Early Pentecostal leader Howard Goss said, "We soon began hearing from scattered, unpastored churches that they had been invaded by the cleverest of confidence men, posing as our preachers."[35] Strange teachings surfaced, and many Pentecostal preachers with little or no formal education did not know how to address doctrinal aberrations.

Problems also cropped up on the foreign mission field, with some missionaries returning home without establishing a lasting work and others seeming to spend most of their time traveling to and from the field. One Pentecostal periodical expressed the general concern when it declared, "We do feel that some have been sent out who should never have gone."[36] Some leaders began to realize the need for some sort of cooperative fellowship that would quell the problems independent churches could not handle on their own.

Against this background, a call was published in the December issue of the *Word and Witness* for a general council to be convened April 2–12 at the Grand Opera House in Hot Springs, Arkansas. The call was addressed to all Pentecostal churches and assemblies "who desire with united purpose to cooperate in love and peace to push the interests of the kingdom of God everywhere." This call came from the leaders of two groups of Pentecostals, one in Texas and one in Alabama, both known as the Church of God in Christ.

The group in Texas had originally been a part of Parham's Apostolic Faith association. When a part of the group decided to sever ties with Parham in 1907, they went to C. H. Mason of the black Church of God in Christ and requested credentials from his organization

since it was already officially incorporated. This new group then adopted the name Church of God in Christ after the name of Mason's network of churches. Legally, they were a white branch of the black organization but functioned independently of it. E. N. Bell, a seminary-trained Baptist from Fort Worth, rose to prominent leadership of this group and was the editor of their paper, the *Apostolic Faith*.

In 1913 the Texas group merged with a small denomination in Alabama with the same name. The Alabama group was led by M. M. Pinson and H. G. Rodgers, both of whom had been baptized in the Holy Spirit through the ministry of G. B. Cashwell. The new organization retained the name Church of God in Christ and appointed Bell to edit their paper, *Word and Witness*. The leaders of this newly formed Church of God in Christ issued the call for a general council of "Holy Ghost" saints in Hot Springs.

BIRTHPLACE OF A FELLOWSHIP

Pentecostal leaders met at the Grand Opera House in Hot Springs, Arkansas, in 1914. The Word and Witness *reported on the meetings and declared "God's Glory Present."*

FIRST GENERAL COUNCIL
Attendees of the first General Council of the Assemblies of God. Front row kneeling (l-r): J. W. Welch, M. M. Pinson, T. K. Leonard, J. Roswell Flower, Cyrus Fockler, Howard Goss, E. N. Bell, and Daniel C. O. Opperman.

In His Own Words

A FUTURE ASSEMBLIES OF GOD OFFICIAL IMPACTED AT AZUSA STREET

Ernest S. Williams, who later served as general superintendent of the Assemblies of God (1929–1949), visited the Azusa Street revival in 1907 and was astounded by what he encountered:

I wish I could describe what I saw. Prayer and worship were everywhere. The altar area was filled with seekers; some were kneeling; others were prone on the floor; some were speaking in tongues. Everyone was doing something; all were seemingly lost in God. I simply stood and looked, for I had never seen anything like it.[37]

Shortly thereafter, Williams received his own personal Pentecost and spoke in tongues. Much later he said:

Soon it will be 59 years since I was filled with the Holy Spirit. I still have my seasons of refreshing from the presence of the Lord, speaking in other tongues and at times shaking under the influence of the Holy Spirit.[38]

All photos courtesy of *Flower Pentecostal Heritage Center*

EXECUTIVE PRESBYTERY
The first Executive Presbytery of the Assemblies of God in 1914, at Hot Springs, Arkansas. Front (l-r): T. K. Leonard, E. N. Bell, Cyrus Fockler. Standing in back: John W. Welch, J. Roswell Flower, Daniel C. O. Opperman, Howard A. Goss, M. M. Pinson.

The convention convened April 2 with more than three hundred in attendance from twenty mostly Midwestern states. About one hundred twenty registered as ministers or missionaries and official delegates. Prominent names in the movement were present: John G. Lake, F. F. Bosworth, J. Roswell Flower, and, of course, Bell, Rodgers, and Pinson. Because many Pentecostals distrusted the idea of organizing, the conveners of this convention set aside the first three days for prayer, worship, and hearing reports and testimonies from those in attendance. This relaxed the tensions and cultivated a sense of unity.

As participants prayed and praised, they felt a distinct sense of God's presence filling the old opera house. One participant recalled a "halo of glory" that rested over the sessions. M. M. Pinson brought the keynote address entitled "The Finished Work of Calvary," which clearly indicated this incipient organization's stance on the controversial subject of sanctification. The Assemblies of God thus represented the formation of the first white, Baptistic/ Reformed Pentecostal denomination. The Assemblies of God would become the world's largest denomination with a global constituency of more than fifty million and an American constituency of almost three million.

ASSEMBLIES OF GOD LEADER
F. F. Bosworth and family in the 1920s.

PREACHERS OF THE WORD
Early Assemblies of God leader Cyrus Fockler (right) with John G. Lake.

ONENESS PENTECOSTALS

At a highly publicized Pentecostal camp meeting in Los Angeles in 1913, one of the speakers noted in passing that the record in Acts indicated that the apostles baptized in the name of Jesus Christ rather than in the traditional formula of Father, Son, and Holy Spirit. One of the attendees, intrigued by what he heard, spent the night studying and meditating on the name of Jesus. In the early morning hours he ran through the camp shouting that God had revealed to him the truth of baptism in the name of the Lord Jesus Christ.

One of those attending the camp meeting was Pastor Frank Ewart, who was profoundly impacted by what he heard. He spent the next year quietly studying the issue and then decided it was time to act. He set up a tent in Belvedere, near Los Angeles, and with another Pentecostal evangelist, Glenn Cook, began preaching that baptism was to be in the name of "Jesus only." They also set up a baptismal tank under the tent and baptized each other according to the newly discovered formula. From Los Angeles, the teaching spread rapidly, gaining adherents and stirring heated controversy.

Along with the doctrine of baptism in the name of Jesus Christ, the Oneness Pentecostals developed a parallel theory of the Godhead that says that the terms "Father," "Son," and "Holy Spirit" refer to the same person in differing modes of existence or relationship.

Just as one person in different relationships may be a father, a son, and a brother, so Jesus is Father, Son, and Holy Spirit, they said.

By 1916 the teaching had gained so many adherents that it was the central issue at the 1916 general council of the Assemblies of God. The council voted for a statement of faith that strongly endorsed the historic doctrine of the Trinity and baptism in the name of the Father, Son, and Holy Spirit. As a result, 156 of the 585 ministers left the organization along with the churches they represented.

The Oneness Pentecostals formed the Pentecostal Assemblies of the World, which is primarily black, and the United Pentecostal Church, which is primarily white. Much later, in 1971, the Apostolic World Christian Fellowship was formed to give unity to the many Oneness Pentecostal churches, fellowships, and denominations. The organization grew to represent 3.5 million people.[39]

NEW DIRECTION
A photograph of what is said to be the first Oneness baptismal service east of the Mississippi River, held in Indianapolis, March 6, 1915. Glenn Cook (left) is rebaptizing L. V. Roberts.

ONENESS FOUNDERS
Frank J. Ewart (right, 1946) and Glenn A. Cook (above, at Murphy Hall in Indianapolis, 1907) began baptizing people in the name of Jesus only, which led to the creation of many Oneness Pentecostal churches and denominations.

AIMEE SEMPLE MCPHERSON AND THE INTERNATIONAL CHURCH OF THE FOURSQUARE GOSPEL

The Azusa Street revival indirectly produced one of the century's most fascinating, dynamic, and famous Pentecostal leaders. Aimee Semple McPherson, born Aimee Kennedy in Ingersoll, Ontario, Canada, was ordained by William Durham at the North Avenue Mission in Chicago with first husband Robert. The couple departed as missionaries to China, where Robert soon died of malaria.

Aimee returned to America and married Harold McPherson of Providence, Rhode Island. In June 1916 they launched into an evangelistic

ministry in churches and auditoriums across America. The grueling lifestyle frayed their marriage, and in 1921 Harold returned to Providence and filed for divorce. The divorce was granted in August of that year.

Aimee continued her ministry and distinguished herself as a powerful and effective preacher. Many said they were miraculously healed through her prayers, and Sister Aimee attracted large crowds as she traveled across the nation. She made the front pages of the newspapers. In Canton the headlines screamed "Cripples Are Cured When Woman

Evangelist Prays." In Denver, twelve thousand people crowded the auditorium every night during her month-long revival crusade there in 1921.

In 1922, while preaching in Oakland, California, Aimee had a vision of Jesus as Savior, baptizer in the Holy Spirit, healer, and coming King. She began to preach what she called "the Foursquare Gospel." Settling in Los Angeles, she built the 5,300-seat Angelus Temple that was dedicated debt-free on January 1, 1923. For three years she preached to capacity crowds every night and three times on Sunday. The following year she became the first woman to be granted a license by the FCC to operate a radio station, KFSG in Los Angeles.

STRETCHER DAY
Sister Aimee prays for the sick.

Aimee founded Lighthouse of International Foursquare Evangelism (L.I.F.E.) Bible College in 1923, and in 1927 the Church of the Foursquare Gospel was established to facilitate the college's growing network of churches and ministers. Aimee continued as president of the organization until her death in 1944. The International Church of the Foursquare Gospel became one of the fastest growing denominations in the world, with 4 million adherents and 38,000 churches in 141 nations.

FOURSQUARE BEGINNINGS
Revival meeting (below) with Aimee Semple McPherson (right detail) held sometime in the early 1900s. Also pictured is Alice Kersey, grandmother of publisher Stephen Strang (left detail). At right, the front cover of Bridal Call Foursquare *magazine, August 1927, and a postcard of Angelus Temple from 1924.*

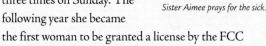

SONGWRITER

Herbert Buffum (immediate left, with family) was one of the leading songwriters of early Pentecost, penning 10,000 songs including the well-known "Lift Me Up Above the Shadows" and "I'm Going Thro', Jesus." Upon his death in 1939, the Los Angeles Times called him the king of gospel songwriters. The Herbert and Lillie Buffum family with Alice Kersey(later Mrs. A. R. Farley) in 1913. The children from left, Naomi, Herbert, Jr., and Ruth. Stephen Strang founder and publisher of Charisma is a grandson of Alice Kersey Farley.
Photo courtesy of *Lorna Medway*

THE REVIVAL ADAPTS AND SPREADS

Early Pentecostals never intended to establish new denominations, but rather envisioned a mighty revival sweeping the entire church, unifying all believers in the power of the Spirit in preparation for the return of Christ to the earth.[40] But by 1914 it was obvious that the revival movement was institutionalizing into denominations, usually defined along racial and doctrinal lines.

In a way, the early divisions in the Pentecostal movement reflected the resilience of the revival and its adaptability to different cultures and doctrinal backgrounds. By 1908, just two years into the revival, the movement had taken root in more than fifty nations. By 1914, Azusa-inspired churches were in every American city of three thousand or more and in every part of the world from Iceland to Tanzania. Pentecostals were already publishing literature in thirty languages.[41]

Early Pentecostals saw this as a spontaneous

The movement grew rapidly and by the 1940s began to capture the attention of the other churches and denominations.

spiritual eruption orchestrated by the Holy Spirit, and it strengthened their conviction that this outpouring of the Holy Spirit would usher in the end of the age and the coming of Christ.

New churches and denominations continued to form, but by 1925 the major racial and doctrinal divides of the movement were in place. The movement grew rapidly and by the 1940s began to capture the attention of the other churches and denominations.

The Rev. E. M. Adams family at a tent revival at Hanna, Oklahoma, in 1925.

PENTECOST SPREADS

M.B. Netzel baptizing a woman at Texas City, Texas, in the 1930s as a large crowd watches from a pier.

GROWTH AND ACCEPTANCE

THE WORLD DID NOT ALWAYS WELCOME PENTECOSTALS AS THEY SPREAD THEIR SPIRIT-FILLED MESSAGE. EARLY PENTECOSTALS WERE RIDICULED, REJECTED, AND EVEN PHYSICALLY ATTACKED. ONLY FOUR DAYS AFTER THE FIRST SERVICE ON AZUSA STREET, THE *LOS ANGELES TIMES* HEAPED SCORN UPON IT. BARTLEMAN SAID, "THEY WROTE US UP SHAMEFULLY."[42] THIS SORT OF DERISION BECAME TYPICAL OF THE EARLY CLIMATE OF HOSTILITY TOWARD PENTECOSTALS. LOCAL LAW ENFORCEMENT OFTEN TARGETED PREACHERS FOR ARREST, USUALLY FOR DISTURBING THE PEACE OR PRACTICING DIVINE HEALING.

CRITIC
G. Campbell Morgan, the "prince of expositors" and longtime pastor of Westminster Chapel in London, called Pentecostalism "the last vomit of Satan."

An account in a 1910 issue of the *Church of God Evangel* told of three Pentecostal evangelists who were falsely arrested in the midst of their tent revival in Alabama.

> They marched us out from our tent and up the street to the stone jail. Immediately they left the jail and returned to the tent, cut it down and set fire to it. While the flames were ascending we were in the iron cells praising God that we were counted worthy to suffer shame for His name.[43]

Ruffians and hoodlums tried to intimidate Pentecostals and disrupt their meetings, throwing rotten fruit, eggs, and sometimes stones at the preacher and his audience. Jewell Nicholson Cunningham, whose father was a Pentecostal preacher in the early days of the revival in Oklahoma, remembered the intense opposition they faced in the town of Bixby, just south of Tulsa.

> Men would come right into the service and yell curses louder than Papa could preach.

Rocks rained on the roof, and a cat was thrown through the window. Somebody threw a rotten egg at Papa while he was preaching, but with his style of preaching he was a moving target and hard to hit. But it got rougher. Shots were fired over the roof and one night a big railroad tie came scooting down the aisle. But we always had a packed church anyway. For those who dared to attend the services, God more than made up for the persecution.[44]

Perhaps the most painful persecution came from other Christians who said that Pentecostal practices, particularly speaking in tongues, was of the devil. In 1912, the well-known Bible commentator H. A. Ironsides denounced the revival as consisting of "delusions and insanities" that cause a "heavy toll of lunacy and infidelity."[45] The well-known Bible exegete and teacher G. Campbell Morgan referred to the revival as "the last vomit of Satan."[46] In 1941, Louis Bauman declared, "The first miracle that Satan ever wrought was to cause the serpent to speak in a tongue. It would appear he is still working his same original miracle."[47] As one historian has said, "It could be asserted that no other religious

expel the Pentecostals, and they eventually found full acceptance within the organization. Soon, Pentecostals constituted the majority of NAE membership.

> "It could be asserted that no other religious movement has suffered more persecution in twentieth-century America, with the possible exception of the Jehovah's Witnesses."

movement has suffered more persecution in twentieth-century America, with the possible exception of the Jehovah's Witnesses."[48]

ACCEPTED BY OTHER EVANGELICALS

Instead of destroying the fledgling Pentecostal movement, persecution seemed to fuel its growth. The sheer numerical size of the movement began to demand the attention and respect of non-Pentecostal Christians. In 1942, Pentecostals were cautiously accepted into the newly formed National Association of Evangelicals (NAE). The NAE was formed as an association of theologically conservative churches who wanted to take a middle road between rigid fundamentalism and liberalism. Although Pentecostals comprised only 10 percent of the attending delegates at the founding meeting, their acceptance stirred immediate controversy. Carl McIntire, founder of the American Council of Christian Churches, offered to merge his organization with the NAE if they would "get rid of the tongues groups." The NAE refused to

ACCEPTANCE BY THE WORLD COUNCIL OF CHURCHES

In 1936, well-known British evangelist Smith Wigglesworth walked into the office of thirty-one-year-old South African David du Plessis and delivered this prophecy:

> I have been sent by the Lord to tell you what He has shown me this morning. Through the old-line denominations will come a revival that will eclipse anything we have known throughout history. You will live to see this work grow to such dimensions that the Pentecostal movement itself will be a light thing in comparison with what God will do through the old churches. You will have a very prominent part. All He requires of you is that you be humble and faithful under all circumstances. If you remain humble and faithful, you will live to see the whole fulfilled.

THE PRAYER OF FAITH
Smith Wigglesworth lays hands on sick child at Angelus Temple in Los Angeles, California, c. 1929.

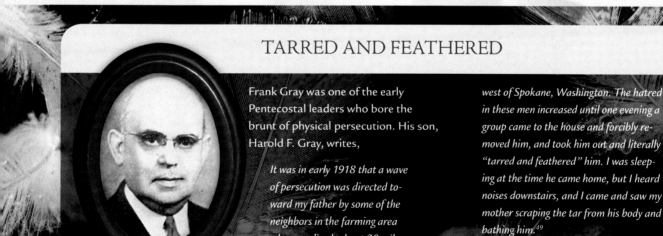

TARRED AND FEATHERED

Frank Gray was one of the early Pentecostal leaders who bore the brunt of physical persecution. His son, Harold F. Gray, writes,

It was in early 1918 that a wave of persecution was directed toward my father by some of the neighbors in the farming area where we lived, about 20 miles

west of Spokane, Washington. The hatred in these men increased until one evening a group came to the house and forcibly removed him, and took him out and literally "tarred and feathered" him. I was sleeping at the time he came home, but I heard noises downstairs, and I came and saw my mother scraping the tar from his body and bathing him.[49]

Frank Gray, 1947

REVIVAL MAY BRING DISRUPTIVE CHANGE

David du Plessis gave the plenary address at the 1948 Pentecostal World Conference held in Zurich, Switzerland. He urged his audience to pray for revival and then exhorted them to be ready for a spiritual upheaval when their prayers were answered. He said, "Nothing can take the place of the Holy Spirit in the church. So let us pray for a greater outpouring of the Holy Spirit than ever before. And remember, when the flood comes, it will not keep to our well-prepared channels, but will overflow and most likely cause chaos in all our programs."

In 1948 du Plessis moved his family to the United States, and in 1952 he became the interim pastor of Stamford Gospel Tabernacle in Stamford, Connecticut. That same year he sensed the Holy Spirit directing him to visit the World Council of Churches (WCC) headquarters in New York City. Du Plessis warily obeyed and was pleasantly surprised when the officials at the WCC received him with open arms and urged him to tell them about Pentecostalism.

Through his contact with the WCC, du Plessis became friends with John MacKay, president of Princeton Theological Seminary and a respected leader

MR. PENTECOST
David du Plessis became an ambassador of Pentecost to liberal and mainline churches

in the WCC. MacKay introduced du Plessis to others in the WCC and arranged for him to attend WCC gatherings and address certain venues. Du Plessis obtained great favor with the WCC and in the following years presented lectures on Pentecostalism at Princeton Theological Seminary, Yale Divinity School, Union Theological Seminary, and other liberal institutions that had been considered off-limits to Pentecostals. His ministry to the liberal churches earned him the title Mr. Pentecost and helped prepare the way for the Charismatic renewal of the 1960s and 1970s.

THE THIRD FORCE

The growing recognition and acceptance of the Pentecostal movement was further highlighted by an article published in the June 1958 edition of *Life* magazine entitled "The Third Force in Christendom." Author Henry Van Dusen, president of the liberal Union Theological Seminary, argued that the incredible growth of Pentecostalism had resulted in it becoming a "third force" in Christendom alongside Roman Catholicism and

UNEXPECTED DEFENDER
Henry Van Dusen (pictured in 1950), president of Union Theological Seminary, called Pentecostals a "third force" in Christendom and defended them against their Christian critics.

Protestantism. He also sharply criticized the traditional churches for referring to the various Pentecostal groups as "fringe sects." "On the fringe of what?" he asked. "Perhaps on the fringe of traditional churches, but not necessarily on the fringe of Christendom." Van Dusen went on to suggest that Peter, Paul, and Barnabas

would probably feel more at home at a Pentecostal revival than in the formalized worship of other churches, Catholic or Protestant.[50]

Social acceptance and affluence, however, seemed to come with a price. As the movement gained acceptance, it seemed to lose spiritual vitality and power. The 1930s and 1940s have been described as a time when "the depth of worship and the operation of the gifts of the Spirit so much in evidence in earlier

> *"...Peter, Paul, and Barnabas would probably feel more at home at a Pentecostal revival than in the formalized worship of other churches, Catholic or Protestant."*

decades were not so prominent."[51] Many were so concerned that they called for systematic times of prayer and fasting to pray for spiritual renewal and revival. The answer to their prayers seemed to be the Healing revival that began in 1946, the Latter Rain revival that began in 1947, and the Charismatic renewal that began around 1960.

THE THIRD FORCE
The growing revival leads to acceptance of Pentecostalism as a third force.

ORAL ROBERTS
Early Oral Roberts' tent meeting.

THE HEALING REVIVAL

VOICES OF HEALING
(l-r) Young Brown, Jack Moore, William Branham, Oral Roberts, and Gordon Lindsay in the 1950s.

WILLIAM BRANHAM (1909–1965) WAS A BAPTIST MINISTER IN JEFFERSONVILLE, INDIANA, WHO MOONLIGHTED AS A GAME WARDEN BECAUSE THE SMALL CHURCH HE WAS PASTORING WAS UNABLE TO SUPPORT HIM AND HIS FAMILY. ACCORDING TO BRANHAM, AN ANGEL APPEARED TO HIM AT 11:00 P.M. ON MAY 7, 1946, AFTER A TIME OF PRAYER AND INSTRUCTED HIM TO CARRY A GIFT OF HEALING TO THE WORLD. THE ANGEL SAID:

> Fear not. I am sent from the presence of Almighty God to tell you that your peculiar life and your misunderstood ways have been to indicate that God has sent you to take a gift of divine healing to the people of the world. If you will be sincere, and can get the people to believe you, nothing shall stand before your prayer, not even cancer.[52]

Branham immediately launched into a limited but successful evangelistic and healing ministry. Jack Moore, a Oneness Pentecostal from Shreveport, Louisiana, saw Branham's potential and gift and introduced him to Gordon Lindsay, an Assemblies of God pastor in Ashland, Oregon. Lindsay, well known and highly respected in Pentecostal circles, agreed to serve as Branham's campaign manager. Lindsay's ability to organize citywide campaigns thrust Branham into international prominence.

THE OPERATION OF SPIRITUAL GIFTS

Gordon Lindsay related an incident that illustrates the operation of the gifts of healing and the word of knowledge in the ministry of William Branham. He said:

In one case I recall that a little deaf boy came to be prayed for. Unfortunately, he was so far back in the line that by the time he got near Brother Branham, the service was closed. The lad and his mother looked so sad and disappointed that Jack Moore turned to me and said, "Why don't you pray for him? So I went ahead and prayed for him and God delivered him. The next day he and his mother were back and they got in the prayer line again. As we saw them in the line again, I looked at Brother Jack Moore and he looked at me. Then he said, "I guess it doesn't do us any good to pray for the people. They aren't satisfied unless Brother Branham prays for them." We watched with interest, nonetheless, to see how Brother Branham would handle the case. When the boy came to him, we were startled to hear him say, "Go your way. A man of faith prayed for you last night and you are healed."[53]

BRANHAM'S CAMPAIGNS
William Branham at the pulpit during a healing campaign in Kansas City, Kansas, April 1948.
Photo courtesy of *Flower Pentecostal Heritage Center*

Branham operated in a particularly powerful ministry of the word of knowledge. When this gift manifested, he often revealed intimate details of the person's life to whom he was ministering. Dr. Walter Hollenweger (1927–), professor of missions at the University of Birmingham, England, served as Branham's interpreter in Europe on several occasions. In his work *The Pentecostals* he writes:

The author, who knew Branham personally and interpreted for him in Zurich, is not aware of any case in which he was mistaken in the often detailed statements he made. It was characteristic of Branham's kind-heartedness that he gave certain personal revelations to those who were seeking healing in a whisper, so that they could not be picked up by the microphone and revealed to the spectators.[54]

One of the most dramatic healings that occurred in the Branham campaigns was that of the former congressman from Georgia, William D. Upshaw. Upshaw's condition was well known, as he had served four terms in Congress and had once run for president. At the time of his healing he had been on crutches for sixty-eight years as the result of an accident that occurred when he was eighteen. Upshaw attended Branham's meetings in Los Angeles, where Lindsay encouraged him to trust God for his healing. Two years later Branham told Lindsay of a vision he had seen of a statesman being healed. The following night, as Branham was leaving the platform, he suddenly said, "The congressman is healed." Upshaw rose to his feet and walked unaided for the first time in sixty-eight years. He later testified, "I laid aside my crutches and started toward my happy, shouting wife... and the bottom of heaven fell out. Heaven came down our souls to greet me and glory crowned the mercy seat."[55]

Photo courtesy of *Flower Pentecostal Heritage Center*

HEALING REVIVAL
Ministers and their wives gather at First Assembly of God in Kansas City, Kansas, in December 1950 for the Voice of Healing convention. Among them, Jack Coe (second row, far left), Freda Lindsay (second row, far right), Jack Moore (third row, far left), David du Plessis (third row, second from left) and Gordon Lindsay (fifth row, far left).

ORAL ROBERTS

About this time, God was dealing with Oral Roberts, a divinity student at Phillips University and pastor of a small Pentecostal Holiness Church in Enid, Oklahoma. In 1935, when Roberts was seventeen, he had been miraculously healed of advanced tuberculosis. God had spoken to him at that time saying, "I have called you to take My healing power to your generation." Now Roberts was diligently seeking God for a fresh outpouring of the Holy Spirit in his own life and ministry and for the fulfillment of that call.

On May 14, 1947, following a seven-month season of focused prayer and fasting, Roberts received an inner assurance that God's call would begin to be fulfilled.[56] At this time, God also revealed to Roberts that he would feel His power in his right hand and that as he laid his hands on the sick, he would be able to detect the name and number of any demons present.

Roberts launched into ministry, emphasizing physical healing and salvation for the soul. His ministry was an instant success. In 1948, to accommodate the crowds, he ordered a tent to seat 2,000. The crowds increased, and by 1953, he was conducting meetings under a tent that seated 12,500. Remarkable miracles occurred, and Roberts became the most prominent healing evangelist of that era.

TELEVISED TENT MEETINGS
Oral Roberts' healing ministry, which began in 1947, helped bring the Healing revival to national attention. Thousands crowded into his tent to participate in meetings and to be healed. Many of his services were televised, and in a very short time Roberts became the face of the Healing revival to millions.

In His Own Words

ORAL ROBERTS' TESTIMONY OF HEALING FROM TUBERCULOSIS

My eldest brother visited me. "Get up, Oral," Elmer said. "I am taking you to a revival meeting where a man is praying for the sick." "I can't get up," I said. "I haven't been able to walk in months." "I'll carry you," he said, and dressed me and put me on a mattress in the back seat of the car he was driving. When the evangelist prayed for me that night, he prayed in the name of the "mighty Jesus of Nazareth" and commanded, "You foul sickness, come out of this boy." At first there was a warmth like warm water coming over me. It went into my lungs. I took a deep breath, and I could breathe all the way down. I knew that a miracle was starting. In a few moments time I was standing straight and tall. I was breathing down deep. I was talking. I was a healed man and in my heart God's voice was ringing: "Son, I am healing you, and you are to take My healing power to your generation."[57]

VOICE OF HEALING

The ministries of William Branham and Oral Roberts signaled the beginning of a significant era of healing evangelism. Almost immediately, a host of other evangelists began reporting miraculous healings and other supernatural phenomena in their meetings. These included A. A. Allen, Jack Coe, T. L. Osborn, William Freeman, W. V. Grant, Kenneth Hagin, and many others.

Lindsay, who separated from Branham in 1955, gave cohesion and publicity to the revival through his *Voice of Healing* magazine and annual Voice of Healing conventions. One writer described his role in the revival as "the conductor of an unruly orchestra."[58]

Jack Coe, c. 1951.   *A. A. Allen, c. 1960.*

Photos courtesy of *Flower Pentecostal Heritage Center*

RESPONDING IN FAITH
A large group gathers at a music hall in Kansas City, Missouri, for the Voice of Healing convention, December 1950.
Photo courtesy of *Christ For The Nations*

FREDA LINDSAY AND CHRIST FOR THE NATIONS

GORDON LINDSAY (1906–1973), who guided the Healing revival during the 1950s and 1960s, founded a Bible school in Dallas in 1970 that he called Christ For The Nations Institute. In April 1973 Gordon died suddenly on the platform of the school auditorium while his wife, FREDA (1914–), was making announcements. The board of directors voted Freda in as president, and under her leadership the school and ministry flourished. Christ For The Nations now sits on an eighty-acre campus in the Oak Cliff section of Dallas. The school offers a two-year institute program and third-year specialty schools of missions, leadership, worship, youth, and children. The ministry is known for its praise and worship recordings and its missions emphasis. Almost thirty thousand students have studied at CFNI. Freda turned the reins of the school and ministry to her son, Dennis, and lives in a campus apartment and serves as president emeritus.

T. L. AND DAISY OSBORN

In 1945, T. L. AND DAISY OSBORN (1923– ; 1924–1995) went to India as Pentecostal missionaries but were unable to persuade people to believe in the Lord Jesus Christ. The young couple returned to America determined to find a more effective way of spreading the gospel. While pastoring in the Northwest they attended a William Branham campaign in their city and saw the power of God at work. After much prayer and fasting, they launched into their own healing ministry emphasizing Hebrews 13:8, which says that Jesus Christ is the same yesterday, today, and forever.

As they began holding evangelistic and healing crusades, signs and wonders followed, and the Osborns believed they had found the right means of spreading the gospel. Following a period of cooperative ministry with the Voice of Healing in America, the Osborns returned to the mission fields of the world. Traveling to seventy-six nations, they pioneered mass healing crusades with phenomenal results. They found that demonstrations of God's compassion and healing power caused thousands to accept Christ in a single service. Their pioneering approach to miracle evangelism became a model others followed in later decades, and it caused the Pentecostal-Charismatic movement to grow rapidly in third world nations where two out of every three Christians would soon identify themselves as a Pentecostal-Charismatic.

MIRACLE MINISTRY
(clockwise from left) T. L. Osborn with a man healed of paralysis in both legs at a 1985 Uganda crusade.
Daisy Osborn with a formerly blind Muslim man who was healed in a Mombasa, Kenya, crusade in 1986.
The Osborns lead a group bearing projectors and film equipment to help them evangelize remote tribes in Papua, New Guinea, in 1971.
The Osborns with a woman healed of blindness at a 1949 tent meeting in Reading, Pennsylvania.
A man holds leg braces and a special shoe he had worn before being healed in a Trinidad crusade in 1965.

ORAL ROBERTS UNIVERSITY

While having dinner in a public restaurant, Oral Roberts heard the voice of God speaking to him, "Build Me a university. Build it on My authority and the Holy Spirit. Teach your students to hear My voice, to go where My light is dim. Their work will exceed yours, and in this I am well pleased." Roberts quickly scribbled the words on a napkin, and they became the central message and mission for the university he would build. Roberts began the university in 1965 and received regional accreditation in a record six years. Dedicated by Billy Graham in 1967, ORU now offers a number of degree programs including liberal arts, business, nursing, communications, and theology. Both graduate and undergraduate schools are now in operation. In the middle of the campus sits the prayer tower with the eternal flame burning at the top, highlighting Roberts' desire for prayer to be central at the university. With an average enrollment of 4,600, ORU is considered by many to be the premier Charismatic university in America. In 1993 Richard Roberts was installed as president of the university, and Oral Roberts retained the title of chancellor.

By the end of 1956, the Healing revival was torn by strife between certain healing evangelists and the Pentecostal denominations to which they belonged. Some strife arose from the denominations' jealousy, but some resulted from some evangelists' questionable practices. The revival waned, and a period of crisis followed for many healing revivalists, causing some to quit the ministry. Among those who continued were Gordon and Freda Lindsay; Oral Roberts, who founded Oral Roberts University in Tulsa; the Osborns; and Kenneth Hagin, who founded Rhema Bible Training Center in Broken Arrow, Oklahoma.

As the Healing revival tapered off, the Charismatic renewal began and soon attracted an even larger and more receptive audience. The Healing revival provided an important link between the Pentecostal movement and the Charismatic renewal. Several prominent leaders from the Healing revival became instrumental in the Charismatic movement.

FATHER AND SON
Chancellor Oral and President Richard Roberts, Oral Roberts University
All photos on this page courtesy of *Oral Roberts University Photography Dept.*

THE LATTER RAIN REVIVAL

Almost parallel with the postwar Healing revival another revival took place—the Latter Rain revival, which began among students and staff of Sharon Bible College in North Battleford, Saskatchewan, Canada. The school's teachers had visited revival services conducted by William Branham in Vancouver, British Columbia.[59] Deeply impressed by Branham's demonstration of the word of knowledge and by the miraculous healings, the community at Sharon began fasting, praying, and studying the Scriptures with heightened expectation. On February 12, 1948, they experienced an unusual demonstration of God's presence and power. Ern Hawtin, a faculty member at the time, describes what happened.

> Some students were under the power of God on the floor, others were kneeling in adoration and worship before the Lord. The anointing deepened until the awe of God was upon everyone. The Lord spoke to one of the brethren. "Go and lay hands upon a certain student and pray for him." While he was in doubt and contemplation one of the sisters who had been under the power of God went to the brother saying the same words, and naming the identical student he was to pray for. He went in obedience and a revelation was given concerning the student's life and future ministry. After this a long prophecy was given with minute details concerning the great thing God was about to do. The pattern for the revival and many details concerning it were given.[60]

The students spent the next day searching the Scriptures for insight and confirmation of the previous day's events. On February 14:

> It seemed that all heaven broke loose upon our souls, and heaven came down to greet us. Soon a visible manifestation of gifts was received when candidates were prayed over, and many as a result were healed, as gifts of healing were received.[61]

Church historian Richard Riss says the events at Sharon raised hope and interest particularly because of the dearth of manifestations in Pentecostalism between 1935 and 1947. The curious and spiritually hungry flocked to North Battleford from across America and around the world. *The Sharon Star* carried reports and advertised camp meetings and conventions. Before long, Sharon faculty members were responding to invitations to minister throughout North America.[62]

LATTER RAIN LEADERS
Sharon Bible College (top, c. 1950) in North Battleford, Saskatchewan, Canada, became a center of the Latter Rain revival. (bottom, l-r) Herrick Holt with Percy G. Hunt and George Hawtin at groundbreaking service for Sharon Orphanage and Schools, c. 1948.
Photos courtesy of *Flower Pentecostal Heritage Center*

NEWS OF REVIVAL
The Sharon Star *was the voice of the Latter Rain revival.*

INCREASE AND OPPOSITION

The revival quickly garnered support. In January 1949, Pentecostal pioneer STANLEY FRODSHAM (1882–1969) visited Bethesda Missionary Temple in Detroit at the invitation of its pastor MYRTLE D. BEALL (1896–1979), who had recently embraced the revival. Frodsham, ordained with the Assemblies of God and editor of the denomination's *Pentecostal Evangel*, was impressed by what he saw and became a supporter of the revival. A number of other well-known ministers and organizations also embraced the revival, including Reg Layzell of Glad Tidings Temple in Vancouver, British Columbia; Ivan and Minnie Spencer of Elim Bible Institute, Lima, New York; Zion Evangelistic Fellowship in Providence, Rhode Island; Lewi Pethrus of Sweden; and many others.[63]

INVITATION TO REVIVAL
Myrtle D. Beall, pictured in the 1950s, was pastor of Bethesda Missionary Temple and an early supporter of the Latter Rain movement.

The revival emphasized the laying on of hands for the impartation of spiritual gifts, the recognition of apostles and prophets in the present-day church, the gift of prophecy for directing and commissioning ministerial candidates, and "proper" church government. These practices, though they had been common among early Pentecostals, were rejected by many Pentecostal denominations.[64] As a result, some ministers, including Frodsham, left their denominations to work as independent ministers or to join loosely formed fellowships. Although rejected by Pentecostal denominations, these Latter Rain believers influenced and were, to a degree, absorbed into the Charismatic renewal of the 1960s and 1970s.[65]

BOLD STEP
Stanley Frodsham, pictured in the 1930s, left the Assemblies of God and his editorship of the Pentecostal Evangel *to join the Latter Rain revival.*

THE FAITHFUL
Camp meeting at Big Bear Lake, California, c. 1936.

THE CHARISMATIC RENEWAL

IN APRIL 1960, TIME MAGAZINE CARRIED THE STORY OF AN EPISCOPAL PRIEST IN VAN NUYS, CALIFORNIA, WHO HAD BEEN BAPTIZED IN THE HOLY SPIRIT AND HAD SPOKEN IN TONGUES WHILE PRAYING IN HIS HOME. DENNIS BENNETT (1917–1992), RECTOR OF ST. MARK'S EPISCOPAL CHURCH, TOLD HIS CONGREGATION ABOUT THE EXPERIENCE AND SUDDENLY BECAME THE PUBLIC FACE OF A NEW PENTECOSTAL-STYLE MOVEMENT TAKING PLACE IN SO-CALLED "HISTORIC" CHURCHES. OTHER NEWS AGENCIES PICKED UP THE STORY, AND BENNETT'S BAPTISM MARKED THE BEGINNING OF THE MODERN CHARISMATIC RENEWAL.

In His Own Words —
...DENNIS BENNETT'S BAPTISM IN THE HOLY SPIRIT

[A]s I spoke on [in tongues] . . . my heart began to get happier and happier! The Presence of God that I had so clearly seen in earlier days to be the real reason for living suddenly enveloped me again after the many, many years of dryness. Never had I experienced God's presence in such a reality as now. It might have frightened me except that I recognized it as the same Presence of the Lord that I had sensed when I first accepted Jesus.[66]

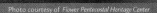
Photo courtesy of *Flower Pentecostal Heritage Center*

Although Bennett had considerable support from within his parish, a small group vehemently denounced his Pentecostal activity. He resigned from St. Mark's under pressure and was assigned to the pastorate of St. Luke's Episcopal Church in Seattle. But the outpouring of the Holy Spirit continued, and by 1963 *Christianity Today* estimated that two thousand Episcopalians in southern California were experiencing the charismatic phenomenon of speaking in tongues.

In a sense, Bennett had been sent to the backside of the desert. St. Luke's was on the brink of extinction, having already been shut down twice. But under Bennett, St. Luke's returned from the dead and flourished, becoming one of the strongest churches in the Northwest and an important center of charismatic renewal for Episcopalians and many clergy and laypersons from traditional backgrounds. As with most *neo*-Pentecostals (as the early Charismatics were called), Bennett promoted speaking in tongues as the initial Bible evidence of Spirit baptism.

Soon, people within most of the historic Protestant denominations were experiencing the gifts of the Holy Spirit. Charismatic prayer groups sprang up across the country, and people sang praises, prayed spontaneously, spoke and sang in tongues, and enthusiastically ministered to one another in the various gifts of the Holy Spirit.

THE CATHOLIC CHARISMATIC MOVEMENT

The Charismatic movement spread to the Roman Catholic Church, where the groundwork had been firmly laid by the Vatican II Council (1962–1965). Pope John XXIII, in calling the Council, said he desired the dawning of a new Pentecost that was "the hope of our yearning."[67] He also directed the churches to pray that the Holy Spirit would renew His wonders "in this our day as by a new Pentecost."[68]

Vatican II Council (1962–1965)

CATHOLIC VOICE FOR PENTECOST

At Vatican II Council, Cardinal Suenens argued in favor of a charismatic dimension in the life of the church. As a result, the Council declared that the charismatic gifts "should be recognized and esteemed in the Church of today."

Vatican II's careful acceptance of those outside the Roman Catholic fold invited new opportunities for interaction with non-Catholic Christians. Instead of using the harsh term "heretic," which had been employed for centuries, it chose the phrase "separated brethren" in referring to non-Catholic Christians. It also declared that Christians of other denominations "are joined with us in the Holy Spirit, for to them also he gives his gifts and graces." These statements opened the way for non-Catholic Christians to lead many Roman Catholics into the baptism in the Holy Spirit.[69]

Equally important was the Council's attitude concerning charismatic gifts. When the subject arose for discussion, Cardinal Ruffini expressed the traditional Roman Catholic view that such gifts today "are extremely rare and altogether exceptional."[70] Contrariwise, Cardinal Suenens pointed out that the charismatic dimension, according to St. Paul, is necessary to the church. These gifts are "no peripheral or accidental phenomenon in the life of the Church"; on the contrary, he said, they are "of vital importance for the building up of the mystical body."[71] As a result of Cardinal Suenens' influence, the Council adopted a receptive position on the *charismata*, declaring that these gifts "should be recognized and esteemed in the Church of today."[72] With this foundation in place, as Synan says, "It was almost inevitable that Pentecostalism would break out in the Roman Catholic Church."[73]

The Charismatic renewal in the Roman Catholic Church began at a weekend prayer retreat in 1967 that was attended by about twenty students and a few professors from Duquesne University in Pittsburgh, Pennsylvania. The weekend gathering was held at a large retreat house known as the Ark and the Dove, and the participants had been asked to read the Book of Acts, John and Elizabeth Sherrill's *They Speak With Other Tongues*, and David Wilkerson's *The Cross and the Switchblade*.[74]

A NEW PENTECOST

Pope John XXIII, in calling the Vatican II Council, directed the churches to pray that the Holy Spirit would renew His wonders "in this our day as by a new Pentecost."

Photo courtesy of *Catholic News Service*

On Saturday evening, after they devoted the day to prayer and study, student David Mangan made his way to the chapel. He later recalled:

> The next thing I knew I was lying prostrate on the floor crying and feeling such "ecstasy" as I may never feel again. I cried harder than I ever cried in my life, but I did not shed one tear. All of a sudden Jesus Christ was so real and so present that I could feel Him all around. I was overcome with such a feeling of love that I cannot begin to describe it.[75]

Later, the entire group gathered in the chapel for what one writer calls "the first totally Catholic Pentecostal prayer meeting."[76] As they prayed, they spoke in tongues, prophesied, and experienced other charismatic manifestations.[77] Synan, who interviewed many of the participants, says:

> As these Catholic seekers prayed through to Pentecost, many things familiar to classical Pentecostals began to take place. Some laughed uncontrollably "in the Spirit," while one young man rolled across the floor in "ecstasy." Shouting praises to the Lord, weeping and speaking in tongues characterized this beginning of the movement in the Catholic Church.[78]

The fire at Duquesne soon spread to Notre Dame University. Many students received the baptism in the Holy Spirit, including Bert Ghezzi, today the editorial director of the Strang Communications book group. From there the movement spread rapidly, and Catholic Charismatic prayer groups sprang up across the country. By 1970, a Catholic Charismatic conference at Notre Dame attracted thirty thousand Catholic Charismatics. Priests, nuns, and laypeople together sang and prayed in tongues, prophesied, and rejoiced in what God was doing.

NOTRE DAME
Notre Dame University became a center for the Catholic Charismatic movement. In 1970, a Catholic Charismatic conference there attracted 30,000 participants.

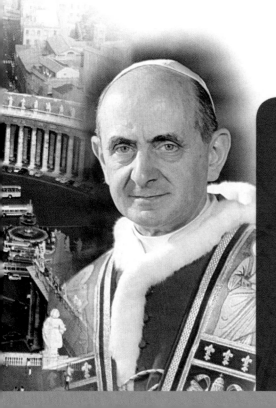

PENTECOSTAL REVIVAL AT THE HEART OF ROMAN CATHOLICISM

The Charismatic renewal in the Roman Catholic Church reached Rome in 1975 where it received the approval of Pope Paul VI. The pope, addressing a gathering of ten thousand Charismatics at St. Peter's Square, pointed to the positive fruit of the renewal and called it "a chance for the Church and the world." He went on to say, "It will be very fortuitous for our times, for our brothers, that there should be a generation, your generation of young people, who shout to the world the greatness of the God of Pentecost."[79]

OFFICIAL BLESSING
Pope Paul VI told a gathering of 10,000 Charismatics at St. Peter's Square in 1975 that the renewal was "a chance for the Church and the world."
Photo courtesy of *Catholic News Service*

CANTERBURY CATHEDRAL

PENTECOSTAL REVIVAL AT THE HEART OF ANGLICANISM

With wide acceptance from the Anglican communion, Anglican Charismatics held an international conference at Canterbury in 1978 to precede the meeting of the Lambeth Conference. Lambeth is the most important gathering of Anglicans, where all bishops meet once every decade. During the week before Lambeth, about five hundred Charismatic leaders gathered at the University of Kent at Canterbury. In the first service, the archbishop of Canterbury and leader of the worldwide Anglican communion, Donald Coggan, addressed the delegates warmly. The closing liturgy was led by Archbishop Burnett and included tongues, prophecies, prayer for the sick, and great rejoicing. This all took place within the context of a traditional Anglican communion service. At the close of this historic gathering, the two thousand worshipers joined in a time of rejoicing as the Spirit was poured out in Pentecostal fullness. Canterbury became for them a new upper room. The ancient walls of the cathedral echoed with shouts of praise. Thirty-two bishops and archbishops danced around the high altar in high praise of the Lord.[80]

PENTECOSTALS AND CHARISMATICS

Many Pentecostals assumed that these "neo-Pentecostals" would affiliate with their churches. But many neo-Pentecostals found acceptance in their own churches and denominations. In fact, the leaders of this movement saw the revival as God's way of renewing existing denominations. For this reason, they encouraged the people to remain within their churches and, for the same reason, preferred the word *renewal* instead of *revival* to describe their movement.

Although new Pentecostals identified with the older Pentecostals in their experience of the Spirit, there were stark differences in their worship styles and views of church and tradition. Since they were not "Pentecostal" in so many ways, the name "Charismatic" became the common designation for this new movement. The difference between a "Charismatic" and a "Pentecostal" is more historical than doctrinal. Those who identify with churches or groups that began at the turn of the twentieth century are considered "Pentecostal." Those who identify with the renewal movement that began around 1960 or those who choose to remain with the older, traditional churches are generally designated as "Charismatic." By the dawn of the twenty-first century, however, the line between the two had become blurred and the term Pentecostal-Charismatic had become the general designation for all who believe in the miraculous, dynamic working of the Holy Spirit in the church today.

ECUMENISM AND SCHISMS

Because of the ecumenical character of the Charismatic Renewal, there was extensive fellowship across denominational lines. Conferences were the order of the day, and conference participants normally represented a healthy cross section of Christendom. Catholic priest and scholar Peter Hocken has referred to the movement as "an ecumenical gift of grace poured out on all the churches."[81]

The high-water mark of the renewal occurred in 1977 when fifty-two thousand Pentecostal-Charismatics met in Arrowhead Stadium in Kansas City. Half the registrants were Roman Catholic; the other half Lutherans, Presbyterians, Episcopalians, denominational Pentecostals, Baptists, Methodists, and Messianic Jews. Great rejoicing filled the stands as the multitude sang in tongues and danced before the Lord.[82]

Although Charismatics were encouraged to remain in their churches, many eventually felt they were withering spiritually while others encountered rejection. Many Charismatics left their denominational churches to join classical Pentecostal denominations or to form new, independent Charismatic churches and fellowships. At least three thousand independent Charismatic denominations have been formed worldwide, and their influence and impact are international.

NEW LEADERS AND INFLUENCES

AS THE CHARISMATIC RENEWAL BECAME ESTABLISHED, MANY INFLUENTIAL MINISTERS AND PASTORS FROM VARIOUS BACKGROUNDS EMERGED IN THE 1960S AND 1970S TO LEAD THE BROADER PENTECOSTAL-CHARISMATIC MOVEMENT INTO A MORE PROMINENT ROLE IN SOCIETY AND THE CHURCH. RALPH WILKERSON (1927–) BEGAN PASTORING A CHURCH IN SOUTHERN CALIFORNIA IN 1961 WITH TWENTY-EIGHT PEOPLE. IN 1969, THEY PURCHASED THE THIRTY-SIX-HUNDRED-SEAT MELODYLAND THEATER IN ANAHEIM AND CONVERTED IT INTO MELODYLAND CHRISTIAN CENTER. IT SOON BECAME A CROSSROADS FOR THE RENEWAL AND HOSTED CONFERENCES, HEALING SERVICES, AND SEMINARS ATTENDED BY PEOPLE OF MANY DENOMINATIONAL BACKGROUNDS. MANY TESTIFIED TO HAVING BEEN HEALED AND BAPTIZED IN THE HOLY SPIRIT THERE. IN 1976 WILKERSON FOUNDED MELODYLAND SCHOOL OF THEOLOGY. J. RODMAN WILLIAMS SAYS, "THE CHARISMATIC MOVEMENT REMAINS INDEBTED TO RALPH WILKERSON FOR HIS VISION AND ENERGY IN MAKING POSSIBLE THESE MEMORABLE OCCASIONS."[83]

KATHRYN KUHLMAN (1907–1976) began her ministry at age sixteen and in 1933 established the two-thousand-seat Denver Revival Tabernacle. After a failed marriage, she settled in Pittsburgh, Pennsylvania. In 1946, in Franklin, Pennsylvania, a woman was healed of a tumor in one of Kuhlman's services, marking the beginning of one of the most heralded healing ministries of the twentieth century. Kuhlman did not have prayer lines, but by the word of knowledge would call out healings that were taking place during the service. In 1965 Ralph Wilkerson invited her to minister at Melodyland Christian Center. For ten years she conducted regular healing services with capacity crowds in the seven-thousand-seat Shrine Auditorium. She also used radio and television to further her ministry before her death in 1976.

Photos courtesy of *Flower Pentecostal Heritage Center*

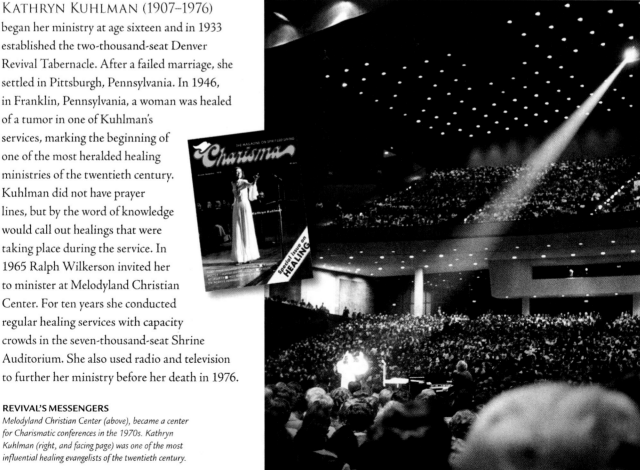

REVIVAL'S MESSENGERS
Melodyland Christian Center (above), became a center for Charismatic conferences in the 1970s. Kathryn Kuhlman (right, and facing page) was one of the most influential healing evangelists of the twentieth century.

LEADERS IN THE PENTECOSTAL-CHARISMATIC MOVEMENT

JACK HAYFORD (1934–) left his post as dean of students at L.I.F.E. Bible College to lead a small Foursquare congregation in Van Nuys, California, in 1969. Through his leadership, the congregation of eighteen members became the ten-thousand-member The Church On The Way, one of America's best-known churches. In 1987 Hayford and The Church On The Way founded The King's College and, later, The King's Seminary. Hayford found wide acceptance among non-Pentecostals and was the plenary speaker at the 1989 Lausanne II Congress on World Evangelism, the only Pentecostal to be afforded this honor. His interdenominational influence has allowed him to build bridges between Pentecostals and evangelicals.[84]

In 1977 ROD PARSLEY (1957–) began a Bible study with seventeen people in Columbus, Ohio, and prayed, "God, please do things so incredibly large and powerful through this ministry that people will have to look past me to You and say, 'No person could have done this.'" The Bible study became World Harvest Church, which meets in a fifty-two-hundred-seat auditorium.

In 1992, Lester Sumrall passed his "sword of anointing" to Rod and his wife, Joni, conferring on Rod the spiritual mantle of his ministry. Sumrall had received the mantle from Smith Wigglesworth by the laying on of hands.

Today, Parsley is well known through his television program, *Breakthrough*. Parsley also founded the Center for Moral Clarity, an advocacy group that some believe helped George W. Bush win reelection in 2004 by turning out Christian voters in Ohio. Parsley's 2005 book, *Silent No More*, issued a rousing call to Christians to become socially and politically active.

In December 1979 TOMMY BARNETT (1937–) accepted the pastorate of the First Assembly of God in Phoenix, Arizona, and grew the church from an average attendance of two hundred fifty to a weekly attendance of fifteen thousand, making it one of the largest churches in America. First Assembly stages elaborate dramatic presentations at Christmas, Thanksgiving, Independence Day, and Easter. Special services conducted between Palm Sunday and Easter Sunday recently attracted one hundred fifty thousand people.

In 1994 Barnett launched the Los Angeles International Church, better known as the Dream Center, in partnership with his son Matthew. The church began with forty-eight people and now reaches thirty-five thousand people per week. President George W. Bush visited the Dream Center and declared it to be a prime example of the effectiveness of faith-based social action.

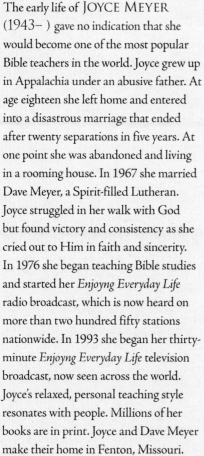

The early life of JOYCE MEYER (1943–) gave no indication that she would become one of the most popular Bible teachers in the world. Joyce grew up in Appalachia under an abusive father. At age eighteen she left home and entered into a disastrous marriage that ended after twenty separations in five years. At one point she was abandoned and living in a rooming house. In 1967 she married Dave Meyer, a Spirit-filled Lutheran. Joyce struggled in her walk with God but found victory and consistency as she cried out to Him in faith and sincerity. In 1976 she began teaching Bible studies and started her *Enjoyng Everyday Life* radio broadcast, which is now heard on more than two hundred fifty stations nationwide. In 1993 she began her thirty-minute *Enjoyng Everyday Life* television broadcast, now seen across the world. Joyce's relaxed, personal teaching style resonates with people. Millions of her books are in print. Joyce and Dave Meyer make their home in Fenton, Missouri.

BILLY JOE DAUGHERTY (1953–) and wife, Sharon, founded Victory Christian Center, now one of the most dynamic churches in North America. Daugherty is known for his emphasis on victorious living through faith in God's Word, divine healing, and world missions. Out of Victory Christian Center has emerged Victory Bible Institute, a large Christian academy, a world missions training center, and Victory Fellowship of Ministries. Daugherty also serves as a board member of the Pentecostal Fellowship of North America and chairman of the International Charismatic Bible Ministries.

Reared in a Jewish orphanage in New Jersey, MORRIS CERULLO (1931–) was supernaturally led to a Christian woman who introduced him to Jesus and the baptism in the Holy Spirit. In the early years of his ministry, Cerullo was associated with the Voice of Healing and became known for his large miracle crusades in third world nations. Cerullo bases his ministry out of San Diego, California, from where he continues to conduct miracle crusades in North America and in other nations.

HEALING TODAY
A Benny Hinn meeting in the Philippines.

THE EVANGELISTS

The 1970s and 1980s also saw the rise of Pentecostal-Charismatic evangelists who drew hundreds of thousands, even millions of people to crusades around the world.

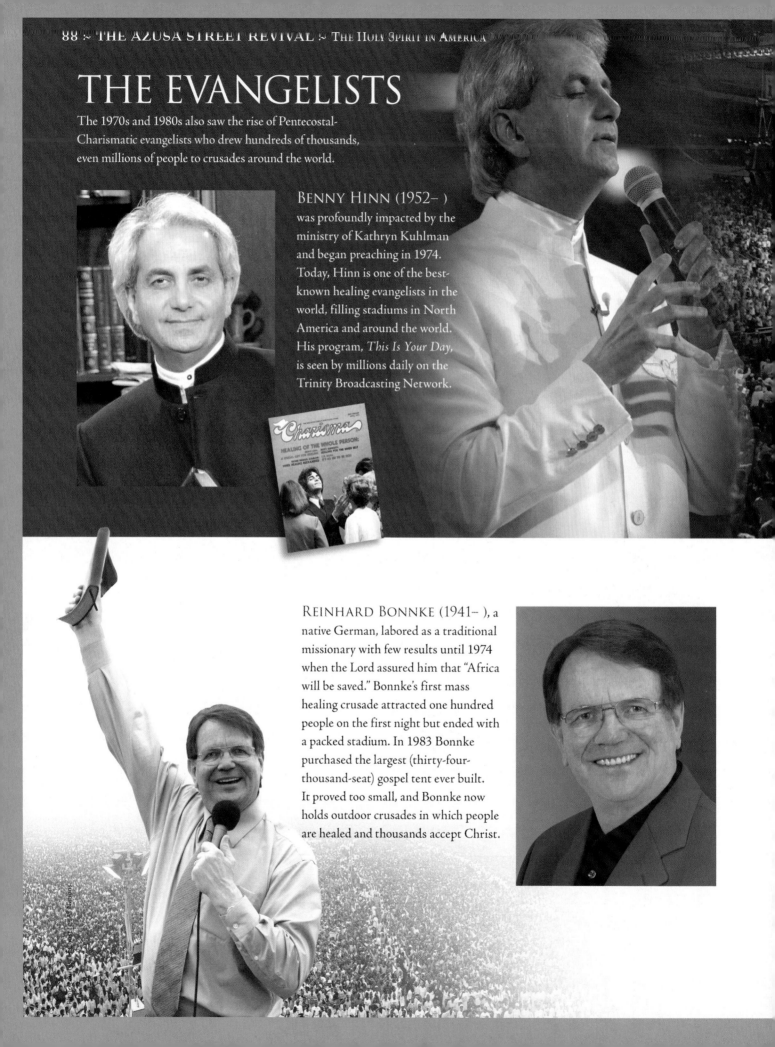

BENNY HINN (1952–) was profoundly impacted by the ministry of Kathryn Kuhlman and began preaching in 1974. Today, Hinn is one of the best-known healing evangelists in the world, filling stadiums in North America and around the world. His program, *This Is Your Day*, is seen by millions daily on the Trinity Broadcasting Network.

REINHARD BONNKE (1941–), a native German, labored as a traditional missionary with few results until 1974 when the Lord assured him that "Africa will be saved." Bonnke's first mass healing crusade attracted one hundred people on the first night but ended with a packed stadium. In 1983 Bonnke purchased the largest (thirty-four-thousand-seat) gospel tent ever built. It proved too small, and Bonnke now holds outdoor crusades in which people are healed and thousands accept Christ.

CRUSADE
Benny Hinn Crusade at Madison Square Gardens

PETER YOUNGREN, (1954–)
a native Swede, established one of the most successful churches and ministries in Canada. Youngren conducts several outdoor mass miracle crusades, which he calls "Festivals of Praise," each year in Africa and Asia.

IBADAN, NIGERIA
*Bonnke's crusades
often draw hundreds of
thousands of people.*

THE WORD OF FAITH MOVEMENT

As the Charismatic renewal spread and left a lasting imprint on the church, another movement arose emphasizing the importance of God's Word as a counterbalance to the experience of the Holy Spirit. The Word of Faith Movement's pioneer was KENNETH HAGIN (1917–2004), a longtime Pentecostal who was healed of an incurable heart disease at age sixteen by claiming God's promises of healing. Hagin taught that the Bible's promises could be appropriated by confessing and acting upon the promise.

Hagin's message of faith in God's Word found a ready audience among Charismatics. While not denying the validity of subjective, spiritual experiences, Hagin and other faith teachers emphasized that the objective truth of God's Word should have priority over any experience. When Hagin and son Ken Jr. founded Rhema Bible Training Center in 1974, the faith message proliferated through its graduates.

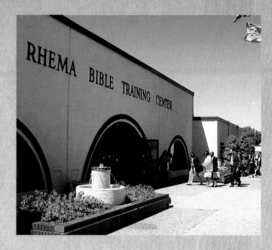

WORD OF FAITH PIONEER
Kenneth Hagin's preaching ministry, Rhema Bible Training Center, and radio broadcasts encouraged millions to live with greater faith.

- THOUSANDS HAVE RECEIVED ACTIVE POSSESSING FAITH!
- A TEACHING MINISTRY WHICH WILL REVOLUTIONIZE YOUR LIFE!
- MIRACLES HAPPEN WHICH CHALLENGE, AMAZE AND THRILL THE SOUL!

A Ministry of Revelation!

HEAR! Kenneth Hagin
BEGINNING DATE — APRIL 18, 1956

The amazing visions and revelations from God

First Foursquare Church
11TH & JUNIPERO AVE.

on:
- HEAVEN
- HELL
- LAST DAYS!

2 Services Daily
Bring The Sick for Healing
10 A.M. - "Faith Clinic"
All Welcome
Nursery Provided for all services.

7:30 P.M.
"Messages of Bible Deliverance"
Prayer for the Sick

FOURSQUARE CHURCH

Dr. and Mrs. Clifford L. Musgrove, Ministers

BLAZING A TRAIL
Many of today's leading ministers were revolutionized by Hagin's teaching on the unalterable truth of God's Word.

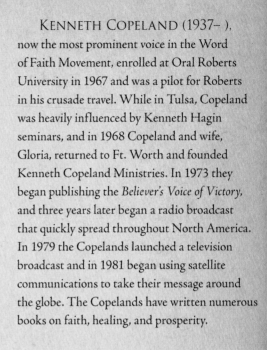

KENNETH COPELAND (1937–), now the most prominent voice in the Word of Faith Movement, enrolled at Oral Roberts University in 1967 and was a pilot for Roberts in his crusade travel. While in Tulsa, Copeland was heavily influenced by Kenneth Hagin seminars, and in 1968 Copeland and wife, Gloria, returned to Ft. Worth and founded Kenneth Copeland Ministries. In 1973 they began publishing the *Believer's Voice of Victory*, and three years later began a radio broadcast that quickly spread throughout North America. In 1979 the Copelands launched a television broadcast and in 1981 began using satellite communications to take their message around the globe. The Copelands have written numerous books on faith, healing, and prosperity.

VOICES OF VICTORY
Gloria and Kenneth Copeland spread the message of faith through their television broadcasts, conferences, books, and tape ministries.

FRED PRICE (1932–) was reared in a Jehovah's Witness environment but was converted to Christ at a tent crusade in 1953. He entered full-time ministry, embraced Hagin's message, and founded Crenshaw Christian Center in the South Los Angeles area. Later the church purchased a thirty-two-acre campus and completed a new worship center called the FaithDome. Price's multiracial congregation is one of the largest in America with more than twenty thousand members. His national television broadcast, *Ever Increasing Faith*, is seen on more than one hundred twenty-five stations.

EVER-INCREASING FAITH
Betty and Fred Price minister at the 10,000-seat FaithDome in South Los Angeles.

PENTECOSTALS DOMINATE THE RELIGIOUS AIRWAVES

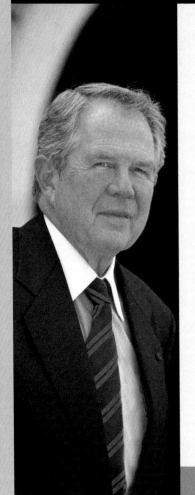

FROM THE TIME AIMEE SEMPLE MCPHERSON PREACHED THE FIRST RADIO SERMON IN 1922 AND ORAL ROBERTS TELEVISED HIS HEALING CRUSADES IN 1954, PENTECOSTALS USED TECHNOLOGY AND MEDIA TO COMMUNICATE THEIR MESSAGE.

CHRISTIAN BROADCASTING NETWORK

One of the most influential religious media outlets to come out of the Pentecostal-Charismatic movement was the Christian Broadcasting Network (CBN) founded by PAT ROBERTSON (1930–) in Portsmouth, Virginia, in 1959. CBN grew dramatically and eventually became a major force in cable television with an estimated thirty million subscribers. In 1989 CBN dropped its nonprofit status and became The Family Channel, a commercial stock-owned corporation. In 1997 The Family Channel was sold to media mogul Rupert Murdoch for a reported $1.5 billion. CBN's flagship program, *The 700 Club*, continues to be seen on The Family Channel and other channels. In 1977 Robertson founded CBN University, now known as Regent University, a widely respected Christian university.

DAYSTAR TELEVISION NETWORK

Daystar Television Network, led by Marcus and Joni Lamb of Dallas, was founded in 1993 with the purchase of channel 29 in Dallas. Daystar now operates forty-five stations in major markets throughout the United States and broadcasts by satellite to two hundred nations.

TRINITY BROADCASTING NETWORK

The largest Christian television network with around 3,334 stations worldwide is the Trinity Broadcasting Network, founded in 1973 by Paul and Jan Crouch. Paul, the son of Assemblies of God missionaries to Egypt, got his start in broadcasting by splicing together tubes and wires to create a campus radio station while a student at Central Bible College in Springfield, Missouri, in the 1950s. There he met Jan Bethany, whose father was the pastor of a prominent Assembly of God church in Columbus, Georgia. Paul and Jan were married in 1957, and Paul began serving on staff at First Assembly of God in Rapid City, Iowa. To supplement his meager salary, he worked as a disc jockey for a country music station. The station owner opened an NBC television affiliate in Rapid City, and Paul conducted the station's first newscast. In 1961 the Crouches moved to California where Paul helped to produce filmstrips and motion pictures for the Assemblies of God and other denominations. He was briefly involved with a local, church-owned UHF Christian station.

In 1973 the Crouches were able, through a series of miracles, to purchase Channel 40 in Los Angeles, and the Trinity Broadcasting Network was born. Thirty-three years later, TBN is on more than six thousand cable systems and reaches ninety-one million American households, representing 90 percent of the U.S. population.

A LIFE IN BROADCASTING
Paul Crouch started a radio station at Central Bible College (top, l-r), then founded TBN, which received its first FCC license in 1974. Today, TBN reaches the world by satellite.

NEW FRONTIERS
TBN now beams the gospel to Russia, the Middle East, Africa, Europe, Southeast Asia, India, Indonesia, Brazil, and more.

WORLDWIDE REACH
Through TBN World Radio and Trinity Music City, USA, the Crouches have diversified and expanded TBN's ministries. Trinity Music City USA in Nashville offers TBN-produced concerts, dramas, seminars, and special events.

Photos courtesy of Trinity Broadcasting Network

CROSSROADS CHRISTIAN COMMUNICATIONS

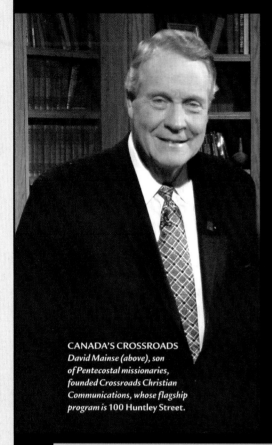

In Canada, Crossroads Christian Communications, Inc., founded by DAVID MAINSE (1936–), produces programming that is seen across Canada and in at least fifty other nations. Mainse, whose parents were Pentecostal missionaries to Egypt, began his television ministry in 1962 while pastoring a Pentecostal church in Pembroke, Ontario. The flagship program of Crossroads, *100 Huntley Street*, is seen daily across Canada by more than one million viewers.

CANADA'S CROSSROADS
David Mainse (above), son of Pentecostal missionaries, founded Crossroads Christian Communications, whose flagship program is 100 Huntley Street.

LEGACY AND FUTURE
Ron and Ann Mainse (above) host 100 Huntley Street. At left (top and bottom), David and Norma-Jean Mainse.

ROBERT WALKER—PUBLISHING PIONEER

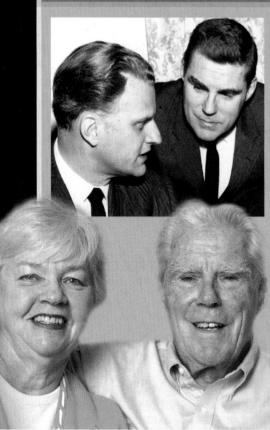

Robert Walker pioneered Christian magazine and book publishing beginning in 1941, when he transformed a floundering publication into *Christian Life* magazine, which became the foremost independent evangelical publication in the United States at the time. It took over other magazines, including *The Way, Religious Digest, Sunday School Digest, Christian Parent,* and *Christian Life & Times,* from which it derived its new name. In 1955, Walker founded *Christian Bookseller* magazine to cover the Christian trade publication industry.

Walker, from the "evangelical mecca" of Wheaton, Illinois, received the baptism in the Holy Spirit in the early 1950s and was one of the first journalists to write about the Charismatic movement. In those years his influence was immense in both religious communities as evangeli-

Walker with Billy Graham (above); Mr. and Mrs. Robert Walker.

cals considered him a Charismatic, while the new Charismatics still considered him an evangelical. In 1968, *Christian Life* profiled Hollywood star Pat Boone and described his experience with the Holy Spirit. Later he published a book by Boone, *A New Song,* which sold an astounding 2.5 million copies in six months to readers hungry to learn more about the work of the Holy Spirit.

In 1987, Walker, then seventy-four, merged *Christian Life, Christian Bookseller,* and Creation House Books with Stephen Strang and *Charisma* magazine. Today, Walker's legacy continues through the many publications and books of Strang Communications. Now well into his nineties, Walker is editor emeritus for *Charisma & Christian Life.* Walker once described the role of the Christian journalist with these words: "We've been born of the Spirit…to communicate the good news of Jesus Christ, of life in the Spirit."

THE THIRD WAVE

In 1983 C. PETER WAGNER (1930–), then professor of church growth at Fuller Theological Seminary School of World Missions, referred to a "third wave" of the Holy Spirit's work that was already stirring in conservative evangelical churches.

The "first wave," Wagner said, had been the Pentecostal revival at the turn of the century; the "second wave" was the Charismatic renewal, which had influenced liberal denominations and Roman Catholicism. This "third wave," Wagner stated, would have a similar impact on the more conservative evangelicals.[85]

JOHN WIMBER AND THE VINEYARD

Along with Wagner, JOHN WIMBER (1934–1997) emerged as a recognized spokesman for the Third Wave. Wimber founded the Association of Vineyard Churches beginning with the Vineyard Christian Fellowship of Anaheim around 1977. Wimber traveled widely to minister in teaching and healing, and his meetings were characterized by manifestations of the Holy Spirit similar to what earlier Pentecostals had experienced: people prophesied, spoke in tongues, were "slain in the Spirit," shook, and swooned in a state similar to drunkenness. While emphasizing signs, wonders, and spiritual gifts, Third Wavers often prefer to remain identified with their own denominations. When asked if he considered himself a Pentecostal or Charismatic, Wagner replied:

> I see myself as neither a charismatic nor a Pentecostal. I belong to Lake Avenue Congregational Church. I'm a Congregationalist. However, our church is more and more open to the same way that the Holy Spirit does work among charismatics....We like to think that we are doing it in a Congregational way; we're not doing it in a charismatic way. But we're getting the same results.[86]

Third Wavers also reject, at least theologically, a subsequent experience of Spirit baptism evidenced by speaking in tongues. They prefer, instead, to see Spirit baptism as part of the conversion-initiation experience. In this approach, every convert has the potential to release any of the spiritual gifts. The genuineness of the experience, however, does not hinge on the manifestation of any particular gift.

Although advocating loyalty to denominations, the Third Wave continues to spawn independent churches and denominations, including the Association of Vineyard Churches, comprising well over three hundred churches throughout North America, and the recently formed Partners in Harvest network of churches, which has formed out of the revival centered in Toronto at the Toronto Airport Christian Fellowship, formerly a part of Wimber's Association of Vineyard Churches.

In spite of the obvious differences among Pentecostals, Charismatics, and Third Wavers, David Barrett, author of the *World Christian Encyclopedia*, sees the Third Wave as part of one great spiritual movement that is sweeping the earth. He says the Pentecostal movement, which began at the turn of the century, the Charismatic renewal, which began around 1960, and the Third Wave are "one single, cohesive movement into which a vast proliferation of all kinds of individuals and communities have been drawn....Whether termed Pentecostals, Charismatics or Third Wavers, they share a basic single experience. Their contribution to Christianity is a new awareness of spiritual gifts as a ministry to the life of the Church."[87]

DOING THE STUFF
John Wimber and his Vineyard churches introduced many people to the gifts of the Spirit.
Photo courtesy of *Flower Pentecostal Heritage Center*

REVIVAL IN TORONTO
Millions traveled to Toronto Airport Christian Fellowship, pastored by John Arnott, to experience the outpouring of the Holy Spirit.

BROWNSVILLE
The glory hits the crowd.

RECENT DEVELOPMENTS

DURING THE 1990S REVIVAL MOVEMENTS SPRUNG UP THAT RESEMBLED THE AZUSA STREET REVIVAL WITH THEIR IN-TENSE WORSHIP, RADICAL OPENNESS TO THE HOLY SPIRIT, AND UNUSUAL SPIRITUAL MANIFESTATIONS SUCH AS FALLING, SHAKING, LAUGHTER, AND WEEPING. PEOPLE CAME BY THE MILLIONS TO THESE NEW CENTERS OF REVIVAL.

"LIKE SOMETHING FROM THE HISTORY BOOKS"
South African evangelist Rodney Howard-Browne, shown at 1993 meetings at the Carpenter's Home Church in Lakeland, Florida, has been an influential revivalist in the United States. His meetings attract thousands.

In March 1993, South African evangelist Rodney Howard-Browne arrived at the Carpenter's Home Church in Lakeland, Florida, for a one-week meeting that turned into a fourteen-week revival. Pastor Karl Strader declared it the greatest move of God he had ever seen, "like something from the history books."[88] Spiritual phenomena such as falling, weeping, and joyous laughter occurred nightly and attracted large crowds. By the fourth week of the revival, fifteen hundred converts were baptized. By the end of the sixth week, cumulative attendance had exceeded one hundred thousand, and many pastors and church leaders were profoundly affected.

After fourteen weeks Howard-Browne closed the meetings, saying that God had shown him that the revival in Lakeland was not to become a mecca, but that he was to carry the revival throughout America. After holding similar meetings at Calvary Cathedral International in Fort Worth, Oral Roberts University in Tulsa, and Rhema Bible Institute in Broken Arrow, Howard-Browne returned to the Carpenter's Home Church in Lakeland for a series of meetings in January 1994. Randy Clark, pastor of a Vineyard church in St. Louis, attended, seeking a new level of spiritual power. Clark was profoundly impacted by what he saw and experienced, which included a burning sensation in his hands.

HUNGER FOR GOD
Randy Clark, a pastor from St. Louis, was seeking a fresh enduement of God's power when he visited a service in Lakeland. God used him to spark the revival in Toronto.

THE TORONTO BLESSING

Shortly after attending the Howard-Browne meetings in Lakeland, Clark went to Toronto, Ontario, to minister at the Airport Vineyard Christian Fellowship pastored by John and Carol Arnott. There the revival that became known as the Toronto Blessing erupted on Thursday evening, January 20, 1994. Characterized by holy laughter, falling, shaking, divine healings, and other spiritual phenomena, this revival soon captured the attention of Christian and secular media. During the first year of the revival, cumulative attendance exceeded two hundred thousand, and people attended from almost every nation.[89] Secular magazine *Toronto Life* billed the revival as Toronto's top tourist attraction of 1994. By the fall of 1997 attendance had reached two million.[90] In spite of concerns about intense spiritual manifestations, many pastors and church leaders testified that their lives, ministries, and churches were transformed by the renewal. The Toronto Blessing was particularly influential in Great Britain where around seven thousand churches, including many Anglican churches, were profoundly impacted.[91] John and Carol Arnott continue as senior pastors of this church, now known as the Toronto Airport Christian Fellowship.

REVIVAL OF JOY
Revival started on a weekday in January 1994 at a service conducted by Randy Clark (right, ministering in Argentina) at a Vineyard church in Toronto, Canada, pastored by John Arnott (below) and wife, Carol. In subsequent years, millions of people journeyed there to experience an outpouring of the Holy Spirit.

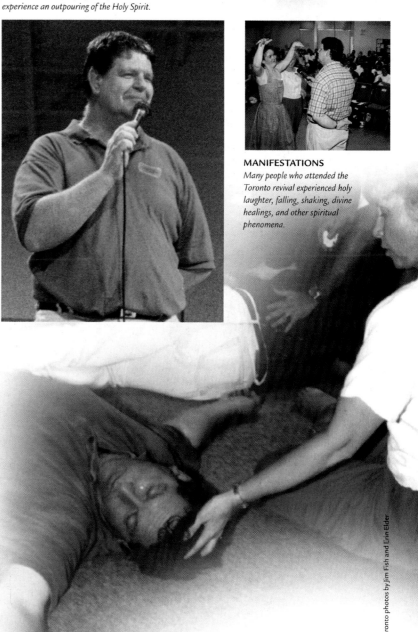

MANIFESTATIONS
Many people who attended the Toronto revival experienced holy laughter, falling, shaking, divine healings, and other spiritual phenomena.

Toronto photos by Jim Fish and Erin Elder

THE PENSACOLA REVIVAL

Another revival with national and international influence began in Pensacola, Florida, at Brownsville Assembly of God on Father's Day, June 18, 1995. Evangelist Steve Hill, who had visited revival centers in Argentina, England,

REVIVAL LEADERS
(l-r) Brownsville Assembly of God pastor John Kilpatrick, worship leader Lindell Cooley, and evangelist Steve Hill.

and Toronto, preached that morning and invited people up for prayer. During the prayer time many people fell to the floor. Among these was Pastor John Kilpatrick, who lay on the floor for more than three hours. He later testified that he felt all the stress drain out of his body. "I couldn't move, but I felt wonderful," he said.[92]

Spiritual phenomena such as falling, trembling, shaking, laughing, and weeping were common in this revival from that day forward. Kilpatrick had been critical of such phenomena, but said the Holy Spirit told him, "John, if you really want revival, don't tell Me how to do it or when to do it. You'll have to step out of the way."[93]

These manifestations attracted much attention and brought a phenomenal influx of visitors to Pensacola from all over the world. At the revival's height, people waited in line for hours to get a seat at an evening service. The revival was covered by the *New York Times*, the *Washington Post*, PBS, and CNN.

THE WORLD'S LARGEST CHURCH

DAVID YONGGI CHO (1936-) is the founder and pastor of Yoido Full Gospel Church in Seoul, South Korea, the largest congregation in the world with more than seven hundred thousand members. Seven services are held each Sunday in the twenty-five thousand-seat auditorium.

Raised in a Buddhist home, Cho converted to Christianity at eighteen when he was healed of tuberculosis after a young woman prayed for him in the name of Jesus. In 1958 Cho and Ja-Sil Choi, who later became his mother-in-law, founded the Yoido Church in a tent left behind by American Marines. By 1964 the original congregation of five had grown to more than two thousand. Overworked, Cho suffered a nervous breakdown, but during his time of recuperation God gave him a plan for delegating ministry responsibilities. As a result the Yoido Full Gospel Church mushroomed in growth and today has fifty thousand small groups that meet regularly throughout the city. Ninety per cent of the congregational growth comes though these groups, where people are baptized, discipled, and pastored. Cho's church has also blazed trails for women in Korean culture: forty-seven thousand of the small groups are led by women and almost two-thirds of his pastoral staff is female.

In 1976 Cho founded Church Growth International (CGI) as a forum for sharing his biblical principles of church growth. Nearly seven million people have participated in CGI seminars. CGI also has a television ministry, a radio outreach, and a publishing arm. Cho is married to Grace (Kim Sunghae) Cho, an accomplished composer and pianist. They have three grown sons and several grandchildren.

THE MEMPHIS MIRACLE

Around the time of the revivals in Toronto and Pensacola, a conference later known as the "Memphis Miracle" took place in Memphis, Tennessee. At this meeting the leaders of the all-white Pentecostal Fellowship of North America (PFNA) dissolved their organization, and a new interracial group was formed called the Pentecostal-Charismatic Churches of North America (PCCNA). Bishop Ithiel Clemmons of the Church of God in Christ was elected the new organization's first chairperson.

The highlight of the meeting came when white Pentecostal leaders washed the feet of black Pentecostal leaders and asked forgiveness for the sin of racism among white Pentecostals. Black leaders then washed the feet of their white brothers in a mutual expression of repentance, humility, and forgiveness. This amounted to a public acknowledgment by Pentecostal leaders that the movement had strayed from its interracial roots at the Azusa Street revival.

Participants in the "Memphis Miracle" saw it as the beginning of a new direction in race relations, especially among classical Pentecostals. Many also saw it as a return to the movement's roots. B. E. Underwood, then general superintendent of the International Pentecostal Holiness Church and co-chair of the Memphis event, declared, "We will return with all our hearts to the unity of the Spirit manifested during the blazing revival at Azusa Street." The meeting received much media attention and raised hopes of a new era of racial harmony and spiritual renewal.

RECONCILIATION

Participants in the "Memphis Miracle" saw it as the beginning of a new direction in race relations, especially among classical Pentecostals.

Photo courtesy of *Flower Pentecostal Heritage Center*

FORGIVENESS

A pastor from Florida spontaneously washed the feet of Bishop Ithiel Clemmons of the Church of God in Christ during the meeting that birthed the racially integrated Pentecostal-Charismatic Churches of North America (PCCNA) in October 1994.

Photo courtesy of *IPHC*

LAKEWOOD CHURCH
Joel Osteen pastors the largest church in the United States, Lakewood Church in Houston.

THE NEXT ONE HUNDRED YEARS

By the beginning of the twenty-first century, the revivals at Toronto and Pensacola had peaked and waned. The crowds became smaller, and revival service schedules were pared back. But the influence of these and other revivals reverberated throughout the church world. Reports of newer Charismatic-type revivals continued to pour in from every corner of the globe. According to Synan, as the twenty-first century dawned, "newer 'Azusa Streets' were popping up in many nations that were spawning mass movements of the Holy Spirit among the masses."[94]

Pentecostal-Charismatics were also moving into positions of influence in society. In 2005, *Time* magazine published a list of what it deemed the twenty-five most influential evangelicals in America. Among them were four well-known Pentecostal-Charismatics: T. D. Jakes, Joyce Meyer, Stephen Strang, and Ted Haggard. Haggard, pastor of New Life Church in Colorado Springs, is also the president of the National Association of Evangelicals and one of the most widely recognized and respected evangelical leaders in America.

Pentecostal-Charismatics have also risen to high levels in U.S. politics. A recent example is John Ashcroft, who served as U.S. senator, governor of Missouri, and attorney general under George W. Bush. Ashcroft is the son of an influential Assemblies of God pastor.

The revival that began in the converted barn at Azusa Street transformed the church forever. Today the Pentecostal-Charismatic movement is growing at a rate of nine million per year. Two-thirds of all Christians in developing nations identify themselves as Pentecostal-Charismatic.[95] Three of the five largest congregations in America are Pentecostal-Charismatic, including Joel Osteen's Lakewood Church in Houston, which has a weekly attendance of twenty-five thousand. Joel is the son of John and Dodie Osteen, who built Lakewood into one of the leading Charismatic churches in the United States, known for its racial integration, worldwide television ministry, and generosity to world missions. Joel continues to build on that foundation. World Changers Church International in College Park, Georgia, is pastored by Creflo Dollar and has a weekly attendance of twenty-three thousand. The Potter's House in Dallas, pastored by T. D. Jakes, has a weekly attendance of eighteen thousand. Four of the five largest churches in the world are Pentecostal-Charismatic, including the mammoth Yoido Full Gospel Church of Seoul, South Korea, which claims more than seven hundred thousand members.

Photo by Steve Chenn

Photo by Billy Bruce

THE LIVING LEGACY OF AZUSA STREET BELONGS TO THE ENTIRE CHURCH, NOT JUST TO THE PENTECOSTAL-CHARISMATIC MOVEMENT. IN THE NEXT ONE HUNDRED YEARS, SHOULD THE LORD TARRY, THE CHURCH HAS AN OPPORTUNITY TO CONTINUE THE WORK OF THE SPIRITUALLY HUNGRY, HUMBLE PIONEERS WHO WELCOMED THE OUTPOURING OF THE HOLY SPIRIT IN THE TUMBLE-DOWN SHACK IN LOS ANGELES, THEN TOOK THAT POWERFUL AND SPIRIT-FILLED GOSPEL TO THE WORLD.

NOTES

1. Vinson Synan, ed. *The Century of the Holy Spirit* (Nashville: Thomas Nelson, 2001), 371.

2. Tertullian, *Against Marcion*, vol. 3 of *The Ante-Nicene Christian Library*, 447, in Eddie L. Hyatt, *2000 Years of Charismatic Christianity* (Lake Mary, FL: Charisma House, 2002), 16–18.

3. J. Roswell Flower, the first secretary-treasurer of the Assemblies of God, in an article adapted from the *Pentecostal Evangel*, January 29, 1956.

4. *The Apostolic Faith*, vol. 1, no. 2, October 1906.

5. *The Apostolic Faith*, vol. 1, no. 1, September 1906.

6. John G. Lake, *Spiritual Hunger/The God-Men* (Dallas: Christ For The Nations, 1980), 13.

7. "When the Spirit Fell in Los Angeles: An Eye-Witness Account," *Pentecostal Evangel*, April 6, 1946, 6–7.

8. *The Apostolic Faith*, May 1907, compiled by Fred T. Corum, *Like As of Fire* (Wilmington, MA: Corum, 1988), 3.

9. "When the Spirit Fell in Los Angeles: An Eye-Witness Account," 7.

10. Lake, *Spiritual Hunger/The God-Men*, 14.

11. Frank Bartleman, *Azusa Street*, ed. Vinson Synan (Plainfield, NJ: Logos, 1980), 60.

12. *The Apostolic Faith*, vol. 1, no. 1, September 1906.

13. Reprinted from the *Los Angeles Times*, April 18, 1906, 1.

14. Bartleman, *Azusa Street*, 59–60.

15. Ibid., 54.

16. *The Apostolic Faith*, vol. 1, no. 3, November 1906.

17. Stanley M. Burgess, ed. and Eduard M. Van Der Maas, assoc. ed, *The New International Dictionary of Pentecostal and Charismatic Movements* (Grand Rapids, MI: Zondervan Publishing, 2002), 366.

18. Gary B. McGee, "William J. Seymour and the Azusa Street Revival," *Enrichment Journal*, Fall 1999, http://www.ag.org/enrichmentjournal/199904/026_azusa.cfm (accessed October 31, 2005).

19. *The Apostolic Faith*, vol. 1, no. 3, November 1906.

20. *The Apostolic Faith*, vol. 1., no. 4, December 1906.

21. McGee, "William J. Seymour and the Azusa Street Revival."

22. *The Apostolic Faith*, vol. 1., no. 5, January 1907, 3.

23. Stanley Frodsham, *With Signs Following* (Springfield, MO: Gospel Publishing House, 1946), 38–39.

24. Stanley M. Burgess and Gary B. McGee, *Dictionary of Pentecostal and Charismatic Movements* (Grand Rapids, MI: Zondervan, 1988), 110.

25. Vinson Synan, "The Unexpected Transformation of the Pentecostal Holiness Church," *Charisma*, April 1987, 55.

26. Hyatt, *2000 Years of Charismatic Christianity*, 148–154.

27. "The Story of Our Church: The Church of God in Christ—Young C. H. Mason," Church of God in Christ, Inc., http://www.cogic.org/history.htm (accessed October 31, 2005).

28. Frodsham, *With Signs Following*, 107–108, in Hyatt, *2000 Years of Charismatic Christianity*, 156–157.

29. Marie Brown, "I Remember," *Pentecostal Evangel*, March 15, 1964, 20, in Hyatt, *2000 Years of Charismatic Christianity*, 152.

30. Edith Blumhofer, *Pentecost in My Soul* (Springfield, MO: Gospel Publishing House, 1989), 244, in Hyatt, *2000 Years of Charismatic Christianity*, 161.

31. Bartleman, *Azusa Street*, 54.

32. Burgess and McGee, *Dictionary of Pentecostal and Charismatic Movements*, 255.

33. Ibid.

34. Ibid.

35. Ethel E. Goss, *The Winds of God: The Story of the Early Pentecostal Days (1901–1914) in the Life of Howard A. Goss* (New York: Comet, 1958), 168.

36. Gary B. McGee, *People of the Spirit* (Springfield, MO: Gospel Publishing, 2004), 112.

37. Ernest S. Williams, "Memories of Azusa Street Mission," Pentecostal Vertical File, Holy Spirit Research Center Oral Roberts University, 1.

38. Ibid.

39. Burgess and Van Der Maas, *The New International Dictionary of Pentecostal and Charismatic Movements*, 940.

40. Carl Brumback, *Like a River* (Springfield, MO: Gospel Publishing House, 1977), 1.

41. Douglas G. Nelson, "A Search for Pentecostal-Charismatic Roots," (PhD Diss., University of Birmingham, England, 1981), Synopsis.

42. Bartleman, *Azusa Street*, 54.

43. Burgess and Van Der Maas, *The New International Dictionary of Pentecostal and Charismatic Movements*, 984.

44. McGee, *People of the Spirit*, 126.

45. Vinson Synan, *The Holiness-Pentecostal Movement in the United States* (Grand Rapids, MI: Eerdmans, 1971).

46. Vinson Synan, *In the Latter Days* (Ann Arbor, MI: Servant Publications, 1984), 77.

47. Ibid., 76.

48. Ibid., 75.

49. Brumback, *Like a River*, 143.

50. Henry Van Dusen, "The Third Force in Christendom," *Life*, June 6, 1958, 122.

51. Carl Brumback, *Suddenly...From Heaven* (Springfield, MO: Gospel Publishing House, 1962), 331.

52. David Harrell Jr., *All Things Are Possible* (Bloomington: Indiana University Press, 1975), 28.

53. Gordon Lindsay, *God's 20th Century Barnabas* (Dallas: Christ For the Nations, n.d.), 176–177.

54. Walter Hollanweger, *The Pentecostals* (Peabody, MA: Hendrickson, 1988), 354.

55. Lindsay, *God's 20th Century Barnabas*, 179–180.

56. Harrell, *All Things Are Possible*, 42.

57. Oral Roberts, *Twelve Greatest Miracles of My Ministry* (Tulsa, OK: Pinoak Publishers, 1974), 13–14.

58. Harrell, *All Things Are Possible*, 57.

59. Richard Riss, "The New Order of the Latter Rain, A Look at the Revival Movement on Its 40th Anniversary," *Assemblies of God Heritage*, Fall 1987, 15.

60. Ibid., 17.

61. Ibid.

62. Ibid.

63. Ibid.

64. See Corum, *Like as of Fire*, Preface, 6, who states that the official board of twelve at Azusa Street would lay their hands on newly approved ministers and pray "as did the apostles of old. People were told where to go on the mission field through visions and prophecy and results followed wherever they went." See also Richard Riss, "The New Order of the Latter Rain," 16, who lists many of the similarities of the Latter Rain movement with the older Pentecostal movement, including the fact that both were known as the Latter Rain movement.

65. Riss, "The New Order of the Latter Rain," 17.

66. Dennis Bennett, *Nine O'Clock in the Morning* (Plainfield, NJ: Logos, 1970), 24.

67. Edward O'Connor, "Roots of Charismatic Renewal in the Catholic Church," *Aspects of Pentecostal-Charismatic Origins*, ed. Vinson Synan (Plainfield, NJ: Logos, 1975), 183.

68. Ibid.

69. Ibid., 185.

70. Francis A. Sullivan, *Charisms and Charismatic Renewal* (Dublin: Gill and Macmillan, 1982), 4.

71. Ibid., 10.

72. Leon Joseph Suenens, *A New Pentecost?* (N.p.: Darton, Longmen and Todd, 1975), 40.

73. Synan, *In the Latter Days*, 109.

74. Kevin and Dorothy Ranaghan, *Catholic Pentecostals* (New York: Paulist Press, 1969), 24. See also Edward D. O'Connor, *The Pentecostal Movement in the Catholic Church* (Notre Dame: Ave Maria Press, 1971), 38–40.

75. Ranaghan, *Catholic Pentecostals*, 26.

76. Synan, *In the Latter Days*, 110.

77. Ranaghan, *Catholic Pentecostals*, 24–37.

78. Synan, *In the Latter Days*, 111.

79. Vinson Synan, *The Twentieth-Century Pentecostal Explosion* (Lake Mary, FL: Creation House, 1987), 49.

80. Ibid., 95.

81. Peter Hocken, *One Lord One Spirit One Body* (Gaithersburg, MD: The Word Among Us, 1987), 87.

82. Synan, *In the Latter Days*, 128–129.

83. Burgess and Van Der Maas, *The New International Dictionary of Pentecostal and Charismatic Movements*, 1196–1197.

84. Ibid., 692–693.

85. John Wimber, *Power Evangelism* (San Francisco: Harper and Row, 1986), 122–135.

86. Ibid., 134.

87. Burgess and McGee, *Dictionary of Pentecostal and Charismatic Movements*, 818.

88. Julia Duin, "Praise the Lord and Pass the New Wine," *Charisma*, August 1994, 24.

89. Daina Doucet, "What Is God Doing in Toronto?" *Charisma*, February 1995, 21.

90. Fred Wright, interview with author, October 1997.

91. Gerald Coates, letter to author, September 18, 1996; Fred Wright, telephone interview with author, August 26, 1997.

92. Bill Sherman, "Pensacola Revival Reaches Tulsa," *Tulsa World*, May 17, 1997.

93. John Kilpatrick, *Feast of Fire* (Pensacola, FL: John Kilpatrick, 1995), 77.

94. Vinson Synan, "Streams of Renewal at the End of the Century," *The Century of the Holy Spirit*, ed. Vinson Synan (Nashville: Thomas Nelson, 2001), 380.

95. David Barrett, "The Worldwide Holy Spirit Renewal," *The Century of the Holy Spirit*, 381–414; and Burgess and McGee, *Dictionary of Pentecostal and Charismatic Movements*, 810–811.

96. See Gary S. Greig and Kevin Springer, *The Kingdom and the Power* (Ventura, CA: Regal, 1993) for a positive evangelical, Protestant view of the *charismata*.

97. Suenens, *A New Pentecost?*, 40.

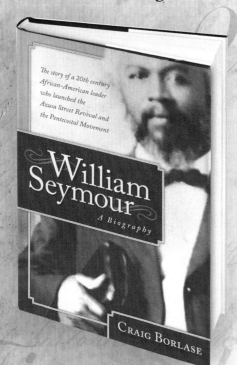
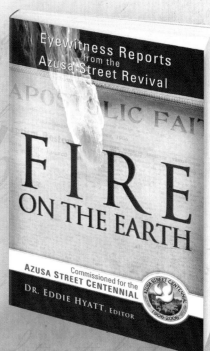
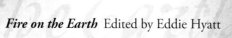